DealSMARTS

Gunter Wessels PhD

Jennifer Bravo

Dedication

Special thanks to all the courageous, hard-working, men and women that make their living in sales. The only thing you can't make more of is time… so, sell well.

Contents

Dedication iii

Acknowledgments vii

Discovery WHY 13

    Best Practices 19

Discovery WHO 23

    Best Practices 30

Discovery WHAT 35

    Best Practices 54

Progression WHERE 59

    Best Practices 66

Progression HOW MANY 71

    Best Practices 77

Progression WHERE ELSE 81

    Best Practices 89

Commitment WHEN 95

    Best Practices 101

Commitment HOW MUCH 105

    Best Practices 118

Commitment WHAT NEXT 125

    Best Practices 134

Summary 139

    Best Practices 142

About The Authors 147

Preface

Here you are reading a book about sales, and you are hoping for some new information. Perhaps you're looking for that secret sauce to take your performance to the next level. Do you have a little time to read about your sales development? We'd like to suggest a different idea about sales.

Simplicity is your friend. Sales must have a linear process, a clear pathway from one step to the next. You can get it right by chance, luck, or habit, but you won't get it right when it counts unless you know what you're doing.

We are probably the only training company in the industry to say this, but we think you already know HOW to sell. After all, you didn't get your sales job by losing a bet! What *might* be missing is the ongoing coaching for continuous development of your prime skills.

Beyond learning the basics of selling, the ability to influence well is in the soft skills. It's the way you frame a decision, ask a question, or the way you follow up with a client. The key to improving your performance is to invest in yourself and learn techniques to increase your skills and effectiveness.

When you put together a puzzle, don't you start by separating the pieces (face up) and then looking at the cover to see what the-end result should be? Of course, how else will you know where to put the pieces? Effective, consistent sales ALSO require you to look at the entire picture first.

In any sales force, whoever is in charge wants predictability, they need a process that works for them, so they train you on their process.

If you are a solo operator, no one is demanding predictability from you, BUT you also need a method for consistency. Ongoing revenue is required and that comes from consistent sales.

Selling goes more smoothly when you use a structured, process-based selling; it improves predictability, win-rates and forecasts accuracy. It's a proven fact that win-rates go from 20-30%, to well over 50% with process-based selling.

Regardless of which process you learn, sales methodology should be simple, something you can hold in your head. It's stuff you already know; you just need a reminder of the process and an easy way to follow it. Just like a pilot uses a preflight checklist, you need a list to make sure you don't miss something important.

Winging it might work if you have put in 10,000 hours and have a lot of experience, but for most of us, *winging it is more like... flinging it,* and rarely produces positive, predictable results.

All the fancy, weird, cool and even old-school sale processes are built on the same basics. The process is simple, every sale has three stages: Discovery, Progression, and Closing. To improve your win-rate, just start in order and work through the stages. If you follow them, you'll always know what to do next.

It really is that simple, a linear process of moving through the stages. It just makes sense that we wouldn't ask for an order before we know WHY the client wants to buy. Trying to close a deal before you've worked through discovery or progression is a bit like wearing your underwear outside of your pants... it's in the right area BUT the order is wrong.

Plan your interactions with the customer. Know where you are in the sales process and do the work in that stage; then close the sale when you have a strong sense of urgency to get the transaction done, by asking them to part with their money.

There's a way to do things that works, the good news is it's simple. You can double your win rate with a process! Your workload can go down while your deal size goes up, your sales cycle is reduced, and your opportunities multiply.

We created this book to encourage you to look at sales from a new perspective and to share some insights we have learned from hundreds of clients. In each chapter we will present a simple concept, teach a skill, help you to change or develop a behavior, and talk about best practices. Once you understand the pieces of the client's puzzle, it's easy to put together YOUR *DealSMARTS℠*.

"The only thing we can't make more of it time, so Sell Well."

-    *Gunter Wessels*

Acknowledgments

Thank you to all the clients, colleagues, and collaborators that made this book possible. Your wisdom and insights have been invaluable in the process.

Introduction

Meet Max! He has just been handed the career-making opportunity he's been waiting for. THIS could be that big deal he's been dreaming of.

Sitting at his desk, head in his hands, Max remembers his first day at Big Idea Corp. He smiles as he recalls meeting his sales manager and boldly informing him, "I'm a born salesperson!" He chuckles to himself as he thinks of the t-shirt he slipped on under his button-up his first day claiming exactly that. *Yup, that's me A Born Salesperson, been there, done that, wore the t-shirt.*

He's been trained on just about every process, has all the skills in the book, yet he's worried about this deal. He looks at the request from Small Think, Inc. on his desk! *This is it! This is the big deal! I've got to get this right!!* Max knows if he wants to close this deal, he and his team need a process - one that keeps everyone on the same page, one that doesn't miss any of the important pieces.

He wanders around the office and gathers together a few members of his team. "Okay, everybody, we really need to work together to get this deal. We need a process. Tell me what you've got."

Steve speaks up first, "Well, I've had some success with the 92-step process, but it can be a bit..." and trails off. Thinking *It sounds complicated,* Max shakes his head and looks at the rest of the group.

"Well, the Hokey-Pokey process is engaging," Chris adds, "but it is easy to get turned around in it." Unwilling to follow a sales process that sounds like a silly dance, Max asks, "Anything else?"

"I know a stellar process," booms Buzz enthusiastically, "the Intergalactic Certified Sales Process." An audible groan rises from the team, followed by eye rolling and obvious squirming.

Max walks away more distraught than he was before. *Everybody's trained on something different. This is never going to work. We need something simple, that we can keep in our heads.*

Max recalls another conversation from his first day at Big Idea Corp. when his sales manager, Dr. Smarts, whose Doctorate in Business Sales hangs proudly on the wall in his office said, "Max, tell me about your sale process," and now Max shook his head at his own reply. "Huh? I don't need that stuff. I'm a natural at this! Believe me, I know what I'm doing."

Knowing where to find an answer, Max headed directly for Dr. Smarts' office as he thought to himself, *I need something now.*

Dr. Smarts motions him in the door, and Max starts right in. "Listen, I know I told you I don't need a process, but everything is riding on this one deal! You've been telling me for a while now that I need to be more systematic."

Dr. Smarts nods his head in sympathetic agreement, he had hoped this day would come.

Max takes a deep breath and continues, "Hey, I guess if anything works, nothing works, but I need something that works! Is there something simple that actually works?"

"Check out DealSMARTS℠," Dr. Smarts sagely replies.

That night, Max tossed and turned in bed until he couldn't take it another minute. *Fine, I'll look at it.*

He logs into his computer, clicks on *insert web address here,* and in the first video he hears," All sales processes are equal; it's really all about what you can hold in your head."

"I knew it!" Max exclaims. *This is brilliant, a simple process for predictable results.* He had finally found the tools he and his team would need, NOW they could all have DealSMARTS℠ and close this deal.

Chapter 1

Discovery WHY

Discovery WHY

They had called and said, "come talk to us," even requesting Max by name. He would have the opportunity to put his new DealSMARTS℠ skills to the test during his first sales meeting with Small Think, Inc.

Max was nervous but excited about the challenge. It was well known the company had always been resistant to big ideas, so why had they called Big Idea, Corp.? Did they understand the products and value Max could offer?

Thinking about his new training, Max jots down some notes for the meeting. *Keep it simple Max, find out what their pain points are, and remember, pain points are personal.* Satisfied with the game plan, Max focuses on other work at hand.

The day arrives, Max was finally meeting with Joe Balow, the head of products at Small Think, Inc. He knows the key to a successful meeting is understanding what's motivating Joe, he'd better figure that out fast.

Joe is apprehensive about meeting with Big Idea, Corp. He believes big ideas are just small ideas glued together BUT the small solutions were not working anymore, and he has heard Max might have some answers to save the day.

Comfortably seated in the conference room, looking down at his papers, Max reads a single phrase, *Discovery Why.* "What's going on with sales here at Small Think, Inc. Joe?" Max pauses to listen for a pain point.

Joe sighs, "Sales are okay, but growth is slow. We have lost some customers, some we needed to lose but some that we regret, and we don't know why they left."

Max knows he needs to dig deeper for answers. "Tell me about these ideas."

"Well, we are selling TryHarder, and our customers that use TryHarder are having great success! But, sometimes, when we recommend TryHarder, our potential customers giggle and say Thanks for Coming! So, we have a new product called TrySmarter!" Joe scans Max's face for a response. "Max, perhaps you can create some new ideas for me!"

It occurs to Max that he still doesn't know WHY Joe is interested, he will need to dig some more to get the whole picture. "So, tell me about the idea lab here at Small Think, and what they have in the hopper."

Joe shifts uncomfortably in his chair and whispers, "We have nothing." He suddenly realizes they are all out of ideas, and his boss can't find out.

Max takes a deep breath and challenges Joe, "I know you have been here for 20 years Joe," Joe quickly corrects him, it's only been 18 years, "What does all of this mean for your legacy, for your family?"

"It's simple Max, I either make the customers happy or I don't get my retirement."

Max quips, "I guess we both need to try harder!"

Almost humored, Joe replies, "it isn't working."

Refocusing on the task at hand, Max continues to dig for information. "What about the rest of the organization?"

"The owners are already looking at Medium Concept, Corp. and there are rumors of a merger. We need production… or we are all gone." Joe looks worried as he fiddles with his pen. "I'm sure there will be a deal, but for us to have any security, we need to be productive."

Digging deeper, Max asks another question. "Joe, what does this mean for your boss?"

"I think he already knows we are running on vapors. He has been acting nervous and stopping by the office to ask about TrySmarter. I have been putting him off, but we are at a point where we can't hide the truth."

Max agrees, "That is scary, what are you going to do, Joe?"

Realizing Max understands the situation, Joe concedes, "As strange as it may sound, we need Big Ideas!"

There it is, Max takes a breath. "Joe, we've been wanting to work with Small Think, Inc. We have management support, and this is an opportunity we want to pursue." He checks off the first item in qualification.

Pausing Max weighs the next question carefully. "Joe, do you want to work with us? Idea Machine is our rival, and they must be interested in working with you. You will certainly need to bring them to the table. So, I need to ask, based on what you know of me and my reputation, do I have your full support?"

Max understands that Small Think, Inc. will still meet with Idea Machine, "Do you think that you need something bigger that what Idea Machine can deliver Joe?"

Joe nods his head, "You have my support Max. We know Idea Machine and they were brought in for what became TrySmarter. They have delivered but we can't execute on what they bring. We need to look at you guys. You have the track record for delivering what we need." Max checks the next box of qualification. They want to work with us.

"Now Joe, this is the hardest part." Max examines Joes expression as he continues, "Do you really think Small Think, Inc. can absorb a big idea? Are the guys in the lab and the rest of your team ready for this? There's a reason you haven't worked with us before."

It is Joe's turn to pause, "I will get them there. We weren't ready before, but we learned that a half-measure approach isn't enough for us."

Not yet satisfied, Max continues, "What about your boss? Small Think, Inc. has been around for 80 years and this is a big shift. I am not sure he is philosophically aligned with moving to a big idea. Maybe you and I think you can make it, but does he think you can make it?"

Joe's shoulders slump, he pauses again, looks around, fumbles with some papers and then sits up and says, "I'll cover that with him and make sure we get that meeting. I will prepare you and you will have to do the rest, but I will get you the audience you need."

Seizing the moment, Max pulls out his calendar and schedules the meeting on the spot. He has discovered Joe's WHY, now it is time to talk to his boss.

"The pain point is personal and emotional - no emotions, no true pain point, no sale."

- Dr. Smarts

Best Practices

Sales trainings often focus on overcoming objections, they are assuming, of course, that the commitment or closing stage is where you *seal the deal*, so to speak. In truth, the discovery stage is far more critical if you hope to accelerate the sales process.

When you really understand your customers reason for buying, you start to build the relationship that can lead to a successful sale.

Consider what you might do if someone approached you in a parking lot and said, "Hey, I'd like to buy to your car." Aside from being a bit creeped out, you would probably wonder WHY they wanted your car.

Even though they expressed an interest in purchasing, your selling position is different depending on their reasons for being interested.

Is your car the same make and year as their first car? Have they dreamed of owning this model but could never find THIS color? Are they a collector, or are they bargain hunting and mistaking you for someone who needs fast cash in exchange for a bad deal? You will never know the potential of the sale unless you take some time for discovery.

There are three things you need to know about every potential sale, WHY, WHO, and WHAT. In the discovery stage of any deal, WHY is the biggest and most important question you can ask yourself.

It can be simple or complex, but the customer's reason for buying is important. More Important than telling them about the amazing features and benefits of your product. In fact, we don't want to break the product manager's heart, but the product is incidental to the sale. The only thing that matters is the customer's pain point and their WHY.

Let's look at how this stage of discovery works. Say you are selling world famous widgets and the market is booming. A customer says, "Tell me about your famous widgets."

In your excitement it can be tempting to blurt out rehearsed lines of features and benefits and gush all over them. After all, you do have the most amazing widgets in the world AND your paycheck is tied to your sales.

Don't do that! Instead practice a pause by inserting a simple question: why? It is a simple step between the request for product information and a nearly volcanic eruption of information from you.

No, not "why do you want to know?" You're not protecting product information from public visibility. Why can sound like you saying, "Great, what's causing you to look at widgets?" The response will guide the conversation as you learn what is most important to THEM.

Why is essential because you are looking for the personal reason they are shopping for widgets. It is always personal, it is NOT about getting information or a general interest. The personal reason is also emotional, and probably negative.

They might be avoiding a problem, concern or fear and gaining something that provides ease or comfort. While getting a good price can be important, it is not their WHY. Price is not a reason to buy. It may be a reason to buy NOW, but it's not the reason TO buy.

If they indicate they are just looking around you could ask, "What features are you looking for in a widget?" As you ask questions and dig deeper, you will find their pain-point or bottom line.

Focus on WHY they want a widget to start with. The more you know about the WHY, the better you're able to make the deal happen in a timely manner.

The first reason you get from the customer is usually just the tip of the iceberg, but you will need to get a picture of the whole iceberg, so you know what you're dealing with. Take the time to dig in and understand your customer and their why, this is where you build the relationships.

As influencing professionals, we earn our money in the discovery process. Why would you sell anything to anyone without knowing WHY they want to buy?

Chapter 2

Discovery WHO

Discovery WHO

Max gathers his paperwork from the table, shaking Joe's hand, "Great meeting Joe, I'll be in touch." He smiles to himself as he heads back to the office. *That DealSMARTS℠ method is working!*

Back at Big Idea, in the comfort of his office, Max composes a follow up note to Joe. *I'd better reinforce this new relationship with Joe and reassure him that I am on HIS team, if I expect him to trust me.*

> Good afternoon Joe,
>
> It was a pleasure meeting with you. Thank you for your time, for your insights, and your support.
>
> I am confident we can make this work as a team. It's important to me that we get this right because I understand the stakes are very high for both of us.
>
> If we work closely on this, we can ensure our mutual success, even if you are forced to go with another company instead of Big Idea, Corp.
>
> I'd like to confirm our appointment next week with Don Wantotock, I look forward to another successful meeting.
>
> Best Regards,
>
> Max

Satisfied with his email, Max sends it off to Joe. *Now, I need to plan the meeting with Joe and Don. WAIT, my process training said I better start by learning more about the rest of the team, so I can keep them involved.*

Max pulls out a piece of paper to start some notes and build a DealMAP℠, this will give him an advantage when it was time to move the sales process along.

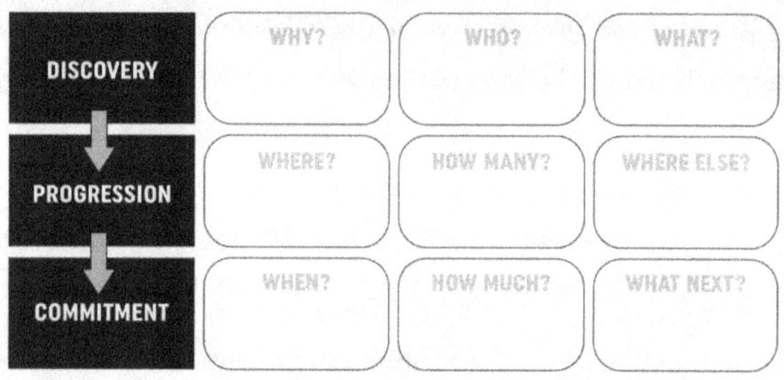

He leaned back in his chair, closed his eyes for a moment, *what do I need to know about the team at Small Think? I need to know what's what, who's who, and what are they going to do, or at least their part in this process. After all, I can't jump over people like an Olympic hurdler and not stub my toe and kick them in the head. I need to navigate these meetings and keep everyone involved.*

Trusty Google was a great place to start mining for information, Max shifted into research mode.

Max thought, *Let's see what I can learn about Don Wantotock.* The only thing online for Don was the standard corporate officers' page on the company website. *He must not be a social media sort of guy.* He looked like a reserved man, but a definite power player! Max made some notes beside Don's name, *High Power - not sure if he is a Promoter or Detractor yet.*

OK, who's next? Not wanting to forget him, Max jotted down Joe Balow on the list. *Probably Low Power but for sure a Promoter.* Max noticed Joe had recently updated his LinkedIn profile, *I wonder if he is looking for a new job already.* He would be an important person in this process, best to keep him close.

Next was Linus Small, who he learned was the son of the founder of Small Think. This was good to know, it meant he was High Power BUT could be a possible Detractor. Sitting on several charitable boards, it was easy to conclude he wants to make a difference. Max would need to get Linus on his side.

Gus Watt, the head of the lab, had an average online presence. He looked like a nice sort with an easy smile. Watching a conference presentation, where Gus was extolling the merits of ideas and deals of all sizes, Max thought, *he is Low Power, but my guess is he will be a Promoter and easy to connect with.* The more the merrier on Team Big Idea!

Finally, there was the VP of Sales and Marketing for Small Think, Dirk Steele. His social media presence was impressive. He was even on Instagram and Snapchat, but his profiles didn't instill confidence. Dirk could be a Detractor and appeared to be Lower Power as well. *Interesting what you can learn on these profiles,* Max mused.

Confident his research has produced some results, Max realizes he still needs more information about the group. *I need clarity on these guys, what do they think they want? What do they really need? What are they worried about?* It was clear that Max needs to have another conversation with Joe.

"Joe, thanks for taking my call," Max was pleased to get through on the first try. "I was hoping you could give me some insights on the team," he paused briefly, "it will really help us to get them on board at our meetings."

Eager to be a part of the solution, Joe provides valuable information about each of them.

"Don just wants results. He is worried the team's lack of performance will create even more of a slow-down," Joe sounded anxious. "He thinks we need more ideas, but he really just needs to see a way forward."

"That's exactly what we are about to give him Joe," Max assured. "Tell me about Linus, the founder's son."

Joe's tone changed, "Of course Linus is also worried about a greater slow down... legacy is much more important to him. He thinks we all just need to stay the current course, so we don't tarnish the legacy. But he never makes decisions alone, and I usually let Don do what he wants.”

Unsure how to respond, Max moves on, “and Gus, talk to me about him.”

Joe is more optimistic, “Gus will be on board for a new approach! He is afraid we can’t get Don and Linus to support it but needs a big idea to run with.”

“Great,” Max takes note, “sounds like Gus is one of us!”

“So, the only one left to talk about is Dirk,” Joe sounds hesitant. “He’s enthusiastic enough, always touting his motivational stuff. Lots of memes come over email from him, but I think he is still trying to prove his value… we brought him in from the nuts and bolts industry.” Max can hear Joe tapping his pen on a hard surface, “he isn’t a fan of TrySmarter, he thinks IF we would give him a bigger budget, he could sell TryHarder just fine.”

Feeling certain he has enough information, Max closes out the call. “Well Joe, I sure appreciate your insights. We have a great team to work with, I am confident we can make this happen.”

Encouraged by the growing rapport with Joe, Max turns his attention to the next task at hand, the meeting with Don. *Ok Max, this is a big one… remember where you are in the sales process and have a plan!*

"Selling shortsightedness is voluntary – you will sell more when you connect with the decision maker, not just the person you are comfortable with, like, click with, or who seems to like you."
- Dr. Smarts

Best Practices

Understanding the power and buyer roles is a critical part of the selling process. You need to figure out who will make THE buying decision, they are the one that can make the transaction happen. But how do you know WHO the decision maker is? The short answer is... you need to be adaptable.

During the WHY Stage of discovery, you learned the personal reasons for each buyer. Finding out who is going to make the decision follows the why very closely.

Traditional sales training will often recommend the direct approach where you simply ask, "who is going to make this decision?" Unfortunately, it usually doesn't add helpful information AND it can feel overly pushy, causing a setback in the sales process.

People like to buy but they hate to be sold. So, we need to make some assumptions to help zero-in on the decision maker.

You can make assumptions about decision making and roles based on a product, sometimes the gender makes a difference, but not always.

For business to consumer transactions, buying housewares or cars for example, the dynamics can be different depending on gender. It can be tricky if you are talking to a man and a woman, they will make a purchase together but one of them is the decision maker.

Regardless of gender, it's reasonable to assume that one of the buyers will think they are the decision maker. It is also reasonable to assume that this belief was given to them by the other person, who is actually going to make the decision.

While you can use stereotypes as a guide to get started, be careful, they can be your fair-weather friend in sales, but if you trust them too much, they may steal your opportunity.

Start the conversation making equal eye contact with both parties, in this way you will keep them both involved without offending one of them. At some point, the decision maker will naturally start to control the conversation and you can identify them safely.

NOW you know who to focus on, but this is not permission to ignore the other person, they still have influence with the decision. If you are dismissive or rude to the companion, they will both walk away from the sale.

In business to business this is easier to navigate, we can assume that the highest role in the organization is the ultimate decision maker so, the bigger the title, the more likely they are THE decision maker. This assumption should be verified before spending too much time focusing exclusively on the person in that role. Sometimes the C-Suite is leading the decision and other times, they are endorsing another role to make the decision.

It's worth considering that the supreme leader isn't always the decision maker. If that person wants something they don't understand much about or it is a product or service used by another team member, they may defer to someone who has their full faith and confidence. Figuring out who the real decision maker is can be complicated in these situations.

Use these criteria to help determine who is who. Once you have assigned roles to each of the people you encounter, you are able to adjust your value proposition to fit the role you are presenting to.

You need to discover who has the motivation and ability to make or break the decision. Who has the motivation but doesn't have the ability to make the decision and finally, who doesn't have the motivation OR ability to make the decision.

Remember, each person has a personal stake in the decision. To move the sales process forward you must focus on how your product or service will serve all the people, be sure to include them.

The people lower down in the organization are the pathway to power. They can get you to THE decision maker faster, so you need to keep them involved.

Getting to the decision maker requires you to gracefully keep the non-decision maker involved.

Chapter 3

Discovery WHAT

Discovery WHAT

Sitting in the impressive executive lobby of Small Think, Inc., Max and Joe start preparations for the face to face with Don Wantotock. "OK Joe let's talk about our objective for the meeting."

"We know Don is aware that something needs to be done but we don't know WHAT he thinks he needs." Max leans in as if to share a secret, "We could get lucky and he will just tell us in his own words, but we can't assume he will hop on board right away. It will be your job to get him to say he wants a solution. Hopefully our solution, but we aren't going to get anywhere if he thinks everything is fine."

Joe takes a deep breath as Max continues, "Joe, if you set the table for him and get Don comfortable, then you can just answer questions candidly and honestly. Remember, I'm the one being inspected here, I will support you and answer any questions you can't!"

Max continues, "Now we need to define what success looks like for us. What do you think will happen Joe, will Don give us the go-sign?"

"Maybe, but he will want the team to buy in and agree," Joe's eyebrows raise slightly in concern.

"Perfect, that's exactly what we want." Max encourages Joe, "We want his permission to dig deeper so when we come back with a recommendation, he knows we have done our homework."

Joe smiles, "that's exactly what Don is going to want."

Satisfied they are prepared for the meeting, both men take a deep breath and sigh.

After a seemingly extended moment of silence, the administrative assistant takes a phone call and without a word, motions them into Don's office.

The office is quiet and impressive. It's spacious with a view befitting Don's station. The large desk situated in the middle of the room and his tall backed chair seem small compared to the massive matching bookcases, full of books, that line the walls. The multitude of awards and a photo of Don with a congressman completes the power statement of the room.

Don is standing, looking out the window with his back to the door. He turns as they enter and motions for them to sit down, "Please have a seat," and they comply.

After a short exchange of pleasantries, Max gets down to business, "Don, I understand you have some concerns about the current performance of TryHarder," Don nods slightly, so Max continues, "And some questions about the new TrySmarter."

Tentatively Don responds, "I'm not sure we need to change anything right now, my team is working on some great ideas, and I'd like to see what they come up with."

"I can appreciate that Don, no reason to change something

if it's working, and you can't rush innovation. But you took this meeting as Joe suggested because you value and support your team, and with your support they reached out to us to explore what we could potentially do for you. To me that means you probably want to know what your options are and what level of change they would require. But to do this right, we need to be clear on what reason there is to consider change. I need to ask, what is that reason? WHAT might make you want a change?" A little nervous about asking a long question, Max musters his most confident look and sits completely still.

Pausing Don seems impressed, "Max, you are the first sales person to ask me that question. The answer is My TEAM. I am running this business and my name is on the line with the board." Don hesitates slightly, "I have some leeway on our direction, but I need to see that my team can execute. If we make a change will it work to make a difference?"

Max gets excited and thinks, *AWESOME,* but then remembers, Don still doesn't know what he needs, *better help him connect the dots*. Leaning in toward Don, "What would your team need to do to show you that?"

Without hesitation Don responds, "Simply come to me and say this BIG Idea works. I need to see them buy in. They are the ones charged with making our success happen. They are the doers. I lead."

"Don," Max inquires, "will that be enough? If they say, we need to go with what Max recommended, will they have your support, or do you need something else?"

Don smiles. "Not entirely Max. They need to underwrite your recommendations, but I really need to see an implementation plan that I can take to the board. If the plan passes my scrutiny, and you have the support of my team, I'm on board." Don looks visibly relieved. "But my approval isn't easy to get. You better know your stuff, and our business, and show me how the plan comes together."

Max pauses, *this is good news!* He realizes that everyone's leadership and reputation are on the line, this is serious. *Good thing we can actually do this stuff,* thinks Max. Big Idea can solve big problems and he will do whatever it takes. *But this isn't enough yet, I need permission to come back and to talk more.*

Thinking about his DealMAP℠, Max shares the list of people he will want to visit and asks, "Is there anyone we missed?"

Don nods, "Dirk, the head of Sales and Marketing, he will want to make sure it fits with our strategy. He understands our culture and is very protective of our people, they ARE the core of this business."

"Perfect, anyone else Don?" Max takes notes and nods.

"You will be talking to Cash later, he handles the contracts." Don is sounding more comfortable and looks relaxed.

Max seizes the opportunity, "It sounds like I have everyone, do I have your support to move forward?"

"Fully," Don stretches out a hand to shake with Max and signal the meeting is concluding, "Linus is right next door, do you want to see him now?"

"Yes Sir!" Max firmly shakes his hand as Don picks up the phone to inform Linus of the meeting.

Joe and Max privately grin at each other as they leave Don's office, feeling satisfied they are making headway.

Slowing the pace, Joe whispers out of the side of his mouth, "Linus means whatever he says," then stepping into his office, Joe makes the introductions.

"Thanks for giving me a few minutes of your time Linus, I'm sure you're busy, so I'll be brief." Max settles into a quick overview of conversation with Don.

"Sounds interesting Max," Linus nods in agreement, "Whatever Don's thinks, I'm on board."

Max thinks as they leave the meeting, *that was short... and strange.* Linus seemed to be genuine, but the very brief meeting left Max feeling unsure that Linus was really on board. He shrugged it off. "Joe assured me Linus means what he says."

Back in his office, Max reflects on the meetings of the morning. *The DealSMARTS℠ process is keeping me on track*, he mused to himself.

Pulling out his DealMAP℠ Max makes another box to add the head of Human Resources, Terri Peoples. He shivers as he writes down her name. *Good grief, I'd better get this right or she will stop everything. Peoples is all about the people. Let's see what we can learn about Terri.*

Max opens a new browser window for some research and discovery. The Small Think website confirms Terri has been with the company for the last five years and her mantra is 'Most companies can achieve what they want by developing their people and letting their talent rise.'

Max pauses, *Interesting.* Further digging on the web reveals Terri is an active member of HRMA, the Human Resources Management Association for HR professionals. She was the former president that advanced the agenda for People First.

Joe had mentioned that Terri was the one to spearhead the initiative to get Small Think on the list of Top 100 Best Places to Work, as rated by People Industry, the HRMA national magazine.

Max considers how Joe and Gus play into the equation. It sounded like a point of pride that there is low turnover in the lab. After all, the lab is a prime resource for Small Think.

If TrySmarter isn't working then performance is likely suffering, which in turn could lead to layoffs. Gus and his team might be getting nervous, and that information would certainly have gotten back to Terri in a survey.

I'm starting to get a picture of our HR leader, Max thought, *she might be resistant to big ideas.* He would need to understand her pain points if he hoped to get HER onboard.

Tapping his pen nervously, Max jots down some possibilities. Lack of business performance. The need to grow talent. Desire to make the top 100 list and get the award. *Think Big doesn't have much to offer her… I need to find a way to tie this to her biggest pain point.* Scanning her online presence again Max exclaims to no one, "It's the award, that's her buy-in!"

Feeling pleased with himself, Max calls the assistant to schedule a meeting with Terri. To his surprise, he gets an appointment right away. *That was too easy… is there something I don't know?* His certainty fades a little, so Max focuses on his plan to win her over. *I must show Terri how we will empower her people, especially the lab.*

What do I know about Terri that will help me create a win-win solution, Max looks back at her list of pain points. If he can show her how it will grow her power base while focusing around engagement in the lab, he can help Small Think transition from TrySmarter to a big idea.

A sudden realization causes a smile to take over his face, Max recalls that Idea Machine is ALL about outsourcing… NOW he has landed on something he can use!

In the waiting room at Terri's office, Max looks around at the motivational posters. He humors himself with the usual jokes, but as the door opens, he realizes he should have been focusing on his questions.

Terri's office is pristine, with an overall sense of power and control. Having learned about behavior styles in his DealSMARTS℠ training, Max knows this indicates she probably has a "D" behavioral style. Max adapts, extending his hand he asks where he should sit. Terri points to the seat in front of her desk. He takes his seat as they exchange pleasantries.

Treading carefully Max transitions the discussion and asks, "Am I right in saying the lab is disengaged currently?"

Without blinking Terri responds, "I'm handling that, what do you have for me?"

Max gulps silently, *all right man Bring it*, "I think you know who we are but if you don't, I can give you a brief summary, our proposal objectives support your goals, including being in the Top 100 Best Places to work."

"Okay." Terri's face softens a little, but her body language still indicates she is guarded.

Good grief, Max paused then continued with an airy voice, "As you know, product performance has a direct effect on employee engagement."

Terri nods slightly, "Yes."

Max takes a breath, "If Small Think can evolve and make a new product work, from your perspective, what impact do you think that would have on your team?"

Now Max has her attention, "That could be a way to fulfill the goal of our organization, employee engagement is the focus of all of our leadership."

A glimmer of excitement in her eyes, Terri continues, "If we pulled together, we could make a new product work, but we would need a solid plan to manage any change. Leadership is concerned right now about change, in fact, I have planned a retreat to give them the tools for change management."

More boldly Max adds, "Without your leadership, any change will lead to disruption. At Big Idea we believe your people are the key to your success."

Terri stops suddenly and looks confused, "Why are you here… we thought you wanted to outsource."

Relaxing, Max realizes they have crossed a barrier. "Outsourcing is not on the table from Big Idea, we don't succeed without your people. We are your partner not an outsource. I can show you how our other clients have been able to leverage their people to make a solution work."

Max continues, "The lab will benefit from our input and when they see how our solutions empower them, you should see an uptick in engagement. I will personally commit to making sure the interaction doesn't miss the goal."

Pausing to collect his thoughts for a bit of a challenge, Max asks, "In your experience where have other partners failed to prepare and enable you to manage this kind of change in the past?" Without waiting for her response Max continues,

"WE need to make sure you are prepared and ready to support an organizational transition – NOT outsource but to a new process and products."

"I know that on the surface big ideas and Small Think, Inc. seem to clash. For this solution to work we need to make sure every member of your team has the tools they need to expand their thinking from Now to Next - not Small to Big." Feeling a little smug Max thinks to himself, *that was pretty good, HA, I should do more crossword puzzles. Look what I did there – Power and Peril of words, WOW, DealSMARTS*^{SM} *training is AMAZING.*

Terri sits quietly, "You said a lot there, and I'm trying to catch up. But I think Matt, what you're telling me is you guys are coming to Don with a solution that does not force us to outsource."

"That's correct," Max reassures her. *I should have stopped talking after asking the question,* thinks Max. *Stupid mistake!*

Looking at him, Terri continues, "Matt, are you telling me you have a good relationship with the lab… my most difficult to manage department?"

Max looks her in the eyes and says, "I do, and they know my name is Max."

Terri blinks and smiles, "Ah. Max, yes. Listening is important isn't it? Well… that's good."

Even though I made a pretty big error here, it doesn't look like I lost her thinks Max. After pausing, to make sure Terri has completed her thought, Max steps into the silence and says, "Terri you have a lot on your plate and this is a big project. I need your support to dig deeper and put this together for Don, what do you need from me?"

"Max," Terri smiles, "I need to see that there is NO outsourcing in your proposal and plenty of employee development. I also like the Now to Next message, I think I am going to borrow that, and you are going to let me take credit for it."

Chuckling Max agrees, "Terri, I like you."

"Everyone does Max," Terri grins at him.

"Do I have your support Terri?" Max pushes a little. As Terri nods her head, and says, "As long as you listen better, we can work together." Feeling a bit bashful Max says, "OK. That's a deal. Thank you for your support."

Terri, clearly feeling more at ease asks, "Who else will you be seeing Max?"

"I'm glad you asked," Max sees an opportunity for more information, "I was hoping to get some coaching points from you for when I see Dirk and Cash."

Looking a little concerned, "Not together I hope," Terri remarks. "They don't play well together."

She continues, "Cash is all about the numbers, sharpen your

pencil because he is a strong negotiator. I hand selected him!" Terri glances out the window and then continues, "Dirk is a good friend of Don's, they play golf together and he is here because Don like his attitude. He is a bit of a challenge with a short attention span but a good fit for his job." She looked sheepish, as though she might have said too much.

Preparing to leave, Max assures Terri that he will return for her approval before submitting the final proposal to Don. Thanking her for the meeting Max thinks, *that was one of the more exciting 10-minute meeting I've ever had. I almost stepped on my own progress!*

Walking down the hall, Max looks for a place to pass some time until his next appointment. Recognizing him from the company website, he sees Dirk standing by the water cooler with some guys, telling jokes.

"Dirk, I'm Max." Introducing himself with an outstretched hand.

"Hey Max… Idea Factory, right???" Dirk grabs his hand and slaps him on the shoulder.

Shocked a bit Max replies, "No, I'm from Big Idea. We have an appointment in an hour, would it trouble you to meet earlier? I know you have a lot on your plate."

"I have an appointment?" Dirk looks confused but shakes it off. "Oh yeah, I love you guys. We have used you for years and your phone systems are fantastic."

Trying to not roll his eyes, Max offers, "That is a different division, but I am here to talk to you about your TryHarder and TrySmarter solutions."

"We are going to nail it with TryHarder," An overly exuberant Dirk exclaims, to no one in particular.

"Do you have a few minutes now – in your office Dirk?" Max tries to steer the conversation toward the coming meeting.

"Sure, let's do it." Dirk leads the way toward his office.

Max follows him down the hall for the longest 30 feet of the day as Dirk greets everyone, encouraging them to visit his Instagram page. *How in world will I get him on board*, Max wonders.

Remembering his DealSMARTS℠ process, Max recognizes the High I traits, realizing that Dirk is likely allergic to details and will have preconceived notions the he will have to get around.

When they finally arrive at Dirk's office, he apologizes for the mess as he clears off a chair for Max. "Please, have a seat, so glad you could come." Without a breath he continues, "I can't wait to hit the water today." Dirk continues and shares a five-minute story about his friend Steve and a golfing trip where they caught fish.

Max jumps in, "Dirk, I like you. I've never heard of a golf outing resulting in fishing. Funniest thing I've heard in a long time. Sounds like you have a lot of fun." Fearing another diversion, without a pause he continues, "thank you for setting aside the time to see me, I would really like to make sure we cover a couple of things."

"Sure, anything man." Dirk puts on a serious face for a moment.

"You're an impressive guy Dirk, and everyone here likes you. Don and the executive team speak highly of you, they're sure you're going to make TryHarder work for the organization." Max can see he will need to work to keep Dirk engaged in the conversation.

Dirk jumps in, "TryHarder... people just don't understand it! When I was in the nuts and bolts industry, we didn't have that solution at first but once I brought it in... it rocked our world! I was a Small Think customer you know. Do you understand how big TryHarder is?" Dirk could hardly contain his enthusiasm.

Dirk continues without a breath, "I'm a TryHarder kind of guy," he lifts a shirt sleeve to show off a lightning bolt tattoo.

Max chuckles to himself, *I really hope I don't see another tattoo, and I'm definitely not getting a Big Idea tattoo.*

Max senses that he is losing control of the conversation fast as Dirk keeps talking, "No one knows what TrySmarter even means." Dirk shakes his head. "The team has been trained on TryHarder, but they don't seem motivated. I have even scheduled special meetings to get more fun into it, but people don't even show up, not even my buddies.

Looking a bit deflated Dirk continues, "Maybe we need some new people or another idea, but that would mean we need to make some tough choices… it makes me sad really."

"Dirk, let me ask you a question," Max attempts to direct the conversation, "how is the lab doing with TryHarder?"

His face brightens, "I like the lab guys! Dan's great… wait not Dan… what is his name again… Gus! We had coffee the other day in the hallway. I keep saying, we need to upgrade TryHarder but Gus can't stop talking about the road block for the next update."

Noting an opportunity Max looks him in the eyes, "Dirk, how do YOU feel about big ideas?"

"That's exactly what I need man," Dirk adjusts in his chair and leans in, "we need a big idea for TryHarder!"

Now we are getting somewhere, Max continues, "Tell me what that looks like for you Dirk."

Dirk shifted into his sales mode, "It's all about the customer, we need to make it fun… that's why I put everything on Instagram, they love that stuff." He continued without a breath, "I know we are Small Think, but our core product is too small, TryHarder is just too small… if we could blend it with a bigger idea, we would be unstoppable!"

Max opened his mouth to speak but Dirk continued, "People think I'm a casual guy, I like to fish a lot, but I know customers. That's why Don brought me in, he understands I have relationships with my customers and I know in my core that if we can expand the formula and make it bigger… TryHarder will take off."

Dirk seems pleased that he came up with the idea to expand TryHarder, "You know who we will need to get on board is Terri, she isn't about making big changes."

Eager to be helpful he continues, "Linus wants to see the numbers come along, I get it… I signed up for big numbers too. Max, if you can help me make TryHarder get bigger with one of your big ideas, I'm in."

Dirk looks down at his phone as it beeps, "Oh man, I have an appointment, I have to go."

Max wonders when he will realize it is with him. "Let's wrap this up. Dirk, I can see a lot of common ground between us. If I can deliver what you're asking for do I have your full support? This must serve you, we will either look good or bad together. I need you to look me in the face and give me your commitment."

"Max, bring me that big idea and I can sell it to the team… you have my support." Dirk stands and shakes hands with his new friend Max.

That was great, Max congratulates himself as he plans his next move.

After learning that Don is out of the country, Max heads

back to his office to send him a summary letter.

"Don, with your support I have collected the perspectives of each one of your leadership team and I am happy to report we have their support."

Max spells out the highlights of the conversations and wraps it up with the next steps, "I will be engaging with Joe and Gus to specify how the solution will fit together and you can expect a detailed proposal in the next 10 days. Once approved we will have a round table meeting about execution. Thank you for your support Don."

Max takes a deep breath and hits send, *I've never closed discovery with a letter, but I have covered my bases. Let's see what Don says.*

"Max, great work and excellent summary. It looks like all the leaders are on board and signs are pointing in the right direction. I know you will come up with something compelling and look forward to your recommendations." Don's email was prompt and Max let out a deep, slow sigh. *Now the real work begins.*

"Ignore the buying criteria you are being measured against at your own peril - find out what the customer thinks they want before you start telling them what they need."

- Dr. Smarts

Best Practices

It is easy to get caught up in the knowledge about your products and services, after all you have done this hundreds of times, you know what you're doing, and you know what solution your customer needs. But don't get ahead of yourself. There is important information missing still. You don't know the buying criteria. You don't know what the customer thinks they need.

It's important to remember that you are still in discovery, you know the WHY and the WHO that has the pain point, but you're not done yet. Don't try to skip this critical step. The WHAT is tied to their pain point, this builds on the previous discovery and gives you the whole picture.

Your customer is not standing there waiting to be fed a solution to their pain point. They *think* they understand your product and their situation. They *think* they know what they need. They are not baby birds, waiting with beaks open, don't be arrogant.

Stop dispensing information for a moment and act like you don't know. Try to use *their* knowledge and understanding of the situation and your solution. As you discover their buying criteria, those things that your product or service must do, it will guide you in offering the best solution for your customer.

In this stage of discovery, you are really doing two things.

First, you need to find out what the customer thinks they need. How can you offer them an effective solution before you understand what they are thinking? This could be very different from what you think they need.

Second, you need to help them find out what they truly need, which includes that stuff they haven't thought about yet. Here you can use your product knowledge and experience to educate them about the choices and benefits they might not have considered.

For a consumer (B2C) sale, the process probably doesn't need mapping, BUT commercial (B2B) sales can always benefit from a DealMAP℠.

A DealMAP℠ is just the process of mapping out the steps that are native in your customers decision-making process.

Once you know HOW they will make the decision, with which criteria, you can start to influence the outcome.

As an example, let's revisit the widget sale from earlier.

You already know who your customer is and that they only want green widgets, but to learn about their native decision-making process and close the sale, you will need more discovery.

Let's map it out.

> *WHO determines if the widget works and will be a good fit for the company?* Let's say Bob is the one that makes that determination. He will run some drop tests to check for durability.
>
> *Great, when will Bob do that?* As soon as Bob gets the sample. (Note: get the sample to Bob)
>
> *THEN what happens?* Bob will pass it on to Steve for flexibility testing.
>
> *Perfect, when will Steve do that?* It usually takes him a couple of days.
>
> *Okay, then what happens next?* Rick will have a look at the terms and conditions of the contract.
>
> *Awesome, when will that happen?* Once Bob and Steve see the widget, it will take two weeks for Rick to look at the contract.
>
> Rick has the final say, yes or no. Done.

The progression of this DealMAP℠ gives you a path to follow for the timing of the sale. WHO decides what, HOW will they decide, WHEN will they decide and what's next in the process.

The WHAT of any deal is the customer's self-generated buying criteria; what they think they need. Once your customer understands what they really need, you have the information necessary to influence them, with style and class you can gently push them into the right solution decision.

The goal for this part of discovery is to get the them to tell you what they really need, in their own words. When your customer says the WORDS then you know you are not making assumptions. Congratulations, your discovery is finished.

Chapter 4

Progression WHERE

Progression WHERE

Tapping his pen on the desk Max reviews his notes on the Small Think deal, *I'm pretty sure Joe and the team have bought into the overall big idea, now I need to get them to take ownership of the solution. Gus will have to OWN this idea for a bigger TryHarder to fully accept that we have a good solution for them.*

Picking up the phone, Max calls Joe to set an appointment, "Hey Joe, Max here. Are you ready to get to work on our deal?"

Joe quips, "Max who?"

Max grins, "Ha! You crack me up Joe… put me on your calendar. By the way, we need to get Gus in on this, is he available?"

"Yes," Joe says chuckling, and then becomes more serious, "Look Max, Gus has been wondering what is going on, he's the one that has to live with this you know."

"Exactly, we are on the same page Joe," Max assures him, "it's time to make sure all three of us are on the same side. I'll see you Monday."

Seated in the executive conference room, Max and Joe exchange weekend war stories about yard maintenance while they wait for Gus to join them.

Gus enters the room, takes a seat, opens his notebook, and looks up at the pair. "Hi," he sounds suspicious and worried, "what do you have for me?"

Max takes a breath and thinks, *here we go... this is not a glamorous part of the deal, but I've got to get him to take ownership while we configure this solution... put your game face on dude.* Max remembers his DealSMARTS℠ process training and recognizes that Gus has a different behavior style, he adjusts his approach and focuses on his pain points.

"Okay, tell me about TryHarder Gus," Max begins, "I need to understand the process, because if we are going to add value, we need to be careful and precise."

Gus visible relaxes at the words, "That would be great Max." For two hours Gus details the process of TryHarder. Max takes furious notes, asking questions often to get clarification.

"Gus," Max takes the conversation back, "It's important to note that we can see the thousands of hours that was put into developing TryHarder. This is important and impressive work you have done. I want you to know, from an outsider's view point, you should be very proud of what you have accomplished. My hope is that we can extend that."

Gus stops cold, with mouth open and there is an obvious pause. "Max, I was convinced you were coming in here to tell me where we were doing things wrong. Everybody has been saying we are doing things wrong, are you telling me you don't think we have been doing things wrong? Don't you have something to sell me?"

Max says with a smile on his face, "You are correct, I'm here to sell you something Gus, but I'm not going to sell you something you don't want… and more importantly I'm never going to recommend something that isn't going to work for you. That's why I needed to understand where you have been innovating and moving things forward. We're not going to undo the good work you've done." Max pauses, "I know you wouldn't support that, and you need to know that I wouldn't ask for that."

Feeling some forward progress, Max thinks back to his DealSMARTS℠ training. He had learned, when dealing with a new buyer that has a different behavior style than his, the new buyer can be uncomfortable with change and somewhat insecure, it's important to keep them calm and at ease… and to recognize their expertise. *Nice job Max,* he thought to himself.

Max did see a lot of good ideas in TryHarder, *there is no cost to showing a customer that you appreciate their work but a lot to gain by getting them on your side.* He had learned this by accident when he had sincerely mentioned to a customer how impressed he was… and it had been his first big deal at Big Idea. Max was starting to feel warm and fuzzy inside, *this was going to be good.*

Continuing Max says, "Gus, tell me about TrySmarter."

Gus fumbles around, pulls out a notebook, and flips through

the pages. "We tried this, we tried this, we tried this..." his words fade off as he mumbles about all the ways they tried to make it work. "No matter what we tried, it conflicted with TryHarder. We just don't have the tools or capabilities to get this thing fixed. It's a bad idea."

Closing the notebook in frustration, Gus slaps his hand down on top and looks square at Max. "You know what, I'm not in marketing but I can tell you that our customers don't want this thing. Our testing data shows that TrySmarter would cannibalize our current business and worse, it would alienate customers. If we go with TryHarder and innovate on that platform, we ARE going to be successful.

Gus continues, "As hard as it was for me to admit at first, the person that understood this best was that guy Dirk. It's amazing, when I met him, I thought he was a complete bag of wind. I don't know what kind of training they get in the nuts and bolts industry, but he gets it."

Looking at Gus and Joe, Max says, "Okay, I have some thoughts, can we discuss those?" Gus pulls out a notepad, prompting Joe to do the same. Max goes to the white board and begins to describe the vision to transform TryHarder with Big Idea's tools.

Max pauses at each point, asking Gus and Joe to comment and getting their buy in at every single point. Max thinks to himself, *it's lucky I know my product so well. Last time I did one like this it took me weeks to prepare. I probably need to prepare for the next meeting a little bit better, but we're in the ZONE and this is going really well.*

Preparing to wrap up the meeting and update his DealMAP℠ Max continues, "I think it's time to summarize and write down our next steps."

Gus puts his hands behind his head, smiles and leans back in his chair, "finally someone said that besides me." The group laughs, everyone is feeling relieved and hopeful.

Max summarizes the next steps, putting together the accountabilities, roles and outcomes for everyone in the organization that will need to contribute to the configuration.

Max concludes, "Let's set up our next meeting so we can discuss How Many of our resources we're going to need to put into this as your partner." Nodding in agreement they set the next appointment.

Max writes down, PROOF, *I am going to need to remember to find some proof statements to support these capabilities before everyone is going to buy into it.*

"Products and services are solutions to problems that are part of a workflow – understand the workflow to position your solution."

- Dr. Smarts

Best Practices

It's always exciting when the deal moves to the progression stage, it feels like the deal is racing toward the finish but beware of a false sense of security! You worked hard during discovery to build value and help the customer learn what they really needed, don't throw it away by skipping some vital information, the buying criteria.

When you thoroughly understand the customer's buying criteria, you are ready to move forward.

The optimistic salesperson might be tempted to skip this step and just use the menu of products and services they offer, telling the customer which one they need, instead of engaging the customer in the process of co-owning and developing the right solution for them. Don't let your optimism blind you. You will only have a satisfied customer if the solution works for them and that means you need more involvement.

Once you know the criteria, it is your job to involve them in the decision making that will lead to the right solution. It is a question-intensive process where the customer evaluates a series of alternatives in the development of a solution. This will create a transfer of ownership of the solution, from you... to them.

This works on any size deal, but let's look at an example of a very simple sale. The principles still apply.

Say a person wants to buy an ice cream cone and you sell ice cream cones! In fact, you have the best ice cream cones in the city. Remember back in discovery you learned that it is always personal. They know they want ice cream, but the WHY is that an Ice cream cone rushes them back to their childhood memories and meets a very personal need for them.

Knowing they want an ice cream cone is just the first step. Now you need to help them decide what that looks like for them. You will need to ask questions to learn more.

Do they want a waffle cone, sugar cone or a cup? What size do they prefer? What flavor do they want? Do they want any toppings? All these things will affect the final price of the ice cream cone. The small vanilla sugar cone is a very different price than the extra-large, 2 scoop, fudge ripple, in a waffle cone with sprinkles ice cream cone will be! How they want their ice cream has a huge impact on their willingness to pay, and their satisfaction.

You need to know WHERE your solution fits into the customers world. Unless you understand their current situation and processes, you won't be able to help them make the best decisions about a workable solution.

More importantly, they need to think it through as well; where does this thing fit into THEIR world? Understanding where to situate the solution is NOT about just you; the customer must gain that understanding too. When they think about where it fits, that starts to create the ownership and proof they will need to buy into the solution.

Intuition, experience, and product knowledge can interfere with your ability to take the necessary time on this step, so be careful or you could blow up your deal by robbing the customer of their opportunity to underwrite the solution.

Also, negotiations always come down to price and configuration (where it fits in). If your customer doesn't quite understand what they are getting or why they are getting it, you might get caught during the configuration process and need to give up on price to make the sale.

Take the time during WHERE and be sure everyone is clear on the configuration before moving to the next step of progression.

Chapter 5

Progression HOW MANY

Progression HOW MANY

Sitting around the large conference table at Small Think, Max opens the meeting with a review of their DealMAP℠, and the progress from the last meeting. Gus and Joe seem eager to take the next steps.

"Okay guys, when you think about TryHarder and the critical elements that need to be changed, where do you see the greatest level of opportunity and risk?"

Without hesitation, Gus and Joe both plop their finger down on the DealMAP℠ on the same spot. Gus speaks up, "It's in the client management process where we have the biggest issue, we just can't seem to be able to close the loop." Joe nods in agreement as Gus explains, "Our clients buy TryHarder, put it to work, and things go well, but if there is a problem, we seem to fumble. This kills our performance and diminishes the value of the solution for our client. We're going to need the most help right there!"

"You know," Gus continues, "what you guys have at Big Idea, now correct me if I'm wrong, would add quite a few resources to this area." Nodding Max assures Gus that he is correct. "It's essential that your solution help us to frame customer expectations, manage delivery on those expectations, and execute follow up communications."

"That's right Gus," Max encourages, "but is it going to be enough for us to just fix that here with a solution, or do we need to scale this and add additional resources elsewhere?

We know how it fits in the workflow but what is the right amount, for performance to be where it should be?"

Joe jumps into the conversation, "We are going to need to expand the budget. I thought we would be able to get this done with a couple of copies of your Big Idea software, but it looks like we are going to need five more modules."

Gus and Joe rapidly discuss what an expanded amount would include. Max struggles to keep up on his notes as they talk about branch offices, partners, headquarters, administration, and even some strategic acquisitions, Max had not even heard about.

Questions are fired at Max from both directions as the men look for clarity on how the solutions will do this or that, and what the technical capabilities are. Max jumps on the phone with product marketing and development many times for answers.

The two-hour strategy meeting turns into a five-hour meeting. *Good thing I didn't have another appointment today,* Max muses in his head, *this is the biggest deal I've ever done.*

Max notices that Gus and Joe are beginning to understand the scale of this implementation and seem a bit disheartened. He asks, "Gentlemen, do we need to get Don into this discussion, so we don't bring him an ugly surprise?"

Reluctantly Joe nods in agreement, "Yes, Don doesn't know how big this needs to be. He's still out of the country but we should be able to get him on the phone."

The secretary puts the call straight through and Don answers promptly. "Guys, I need some good news, we have a lot of opportunity here, tell me you are getting somewhere."

Joe speaks up, "We are, but the solutions is going to need to be bigger than we thought."

Don pauses for a second, "How much bigger?" Gus and Joe look at each other nervously, each wait for the other to speak.

"Don, Max here," Max jumps in, "these guys have done their due diligence and conservatively we are going to need to scale this up by five more modules." The silence in the room deafening.

Finally, Don speaks, "That's what I thought. You guys are always trying to fix things with an overly-conservative solution. Either we need to take a big leap into TrySmarter or we need to fix TryHarder. I never believed we could get this done as quickly and cheaply as you guys said."

Don continues as the air slowly returns to the room, "I need this commitment from you guys. If we put the right level of resources behind you, will you be able to execute? This has us ALL on the line."

The group nervously look at each other and Joe says, "Without a doubt, we will get it done. We are grateful for your support."

Don replies abruptly, "Good." And the call is over.

With deep breaths the group is relieved to have the added resources and is feeling optimistic. Turning their attention back to the DealMAP℠, Max assigns new accountabilities, responsibilities and timing to the now expanded project.

Max agrees to update the configuration on the proposal draft and packs up to leave.

"You heard Don," Gus stands and looks Max in the eye, "we're all on the line here. I need to see how this will work. Can you show me how others have done this, because I can't quite see it yet."

Joe weighs in, "I couldn't agree more, we are going to need to show EVERYONE that the plan we are coming up with is strong."

Max smiles, "I'm already working on just that for you guys. At our next meeting, we will talk about how others have done this.

Smiles and handshakes all around, the meeting is over.

"Goldilocks was a bad salesperson - right-size your solution because YOU don't have three chances."

Dr. Smarts

Best Practices

Selling is not for amateurs, you need to know what you're doing. There must be respect for the customer, respect for the process, and respect for the outcome.

As a sales person, it is your job to guide the customer through the sales process with product and utilization information. During progression you are managing the deal, the process of them taking ownership, as you solidify their understanding of the why, who, and what of discovery.

During discovery you made sure the client was in touch with their pain points. Those primarily negative emotions they have because they are unhappy with something they want to fix. They are motivated to find a solution.

In progression you maintain and feed that motivation with facts, figures, and details which drive their understanding with appropriate information.

As you learn about their situation and they learn about your solution, sometimes the solution might need to change. *How many* is just the part of the process and you need to figure out where they need it, what else they really need and the value it brings. The customer saw this in discovery but NOW they are listening with new ears!

During the discussion about how many of your products or services they will need, you must free yourself from thinking you got it right out of the gate. Be mindful that you can be trapped in your own thinking about size and scope. You can trap yourself by under-estimating the size and scale of the problem or overestimate your ability to fix it.

Additionally, you might artificially think you need to do this *cheap* for the customer. This is a problem. Big solutions are expensive. Organizations that have big problems, want big solutions and they are willing to invest for real outcomes.

Assumptions about competitors and needed differentiation can't drive the configuration of the solutions either. Be careful not to over stuff the solution with things that don't matter. Let the customer make the solution their own and get their fingerprints on it. This creates more buy-in, which will lead to better outcomes and win rates.

As a sales professional you might think of the deal as YOUR

sale, but in truth, the customer takes the solution from the sales person. The customer is making the decision and you are supporting the process. Your job is to influence them and guide them toward the best solution for THEM.

Be careful not to injure your deal after you made it so strong in discovery. Using a standard solution when a tailored solution is the best answer means you're begging to have your price questioned, you're begging to have your value proposition diminished, and you're begging to have a problem later.

All solutions are tailored and configured during the progression phase of the sale meaning it is customized for the specific needs of the customer. Every deal deserves your diligent focus during this phase. The right solution will perform better, be more profitable and will maximize customer satisfaction.

Your only job during progression is to get the deal dialed-in and get the buy-in for the solution. They have already argued with themselves about what the solution is or isn't and how it will work. If you've done your progression job well, the customer *gets* what they are buying because they had a hand in the process. Buy-in and proof will be less rigorous because you involved them.

Chapter 6

Progression WHERE ELSE

Progression WHERE ELSE

Walking into the Small Think, Inc. headquarters, Max muses, *my briefcase is heavy today. I don't think this has ever happened in my career, I have case studies and references that fit this solution perfectly. I have even impressed myself!* Humored by his thoughts Max smiles, *everyone dreams of these days and now I'm having one, this calls for a celebration later.*

Sitting down at the now familiar conference table, Max shares the excitement of the weekend. "The neighborhood party got a bit out of hand and my oldest son almost had his first arrest experience!" Chuckling he added, "Kids, what are you going to do?"

Gus joins the war stories with the adventures of sick kids at his house.

Max remembers he forgot to pack his hand sanitizer as he rubs his right hand on his pant leg under the table.

Max gets the meeting started. "Okay guys, we have mapped it out, we've got accountabilities, let's do a process check. Where are we?"

"Well," Joe glances at Gus, "what we need to see now is something we can take forward to the team that supports this recommendation. Thankfully, Don recognizes that this needs to be bigger, but he will want to see some proof and frankly, so do we."

Max jokes, "Well, we've been working on time travel in my garage, and we are getting close, but I have lost a lot of friends. We are pretty confident this next try is going to work, so we are thinking this might be our chance. You guys ready to volunteer?" Seeing the expressions on their faces, Max immediately regrets the joke.

Gus purses his lips, "It needs to be objective, hard evidence for me to sign off on this. I am risking my reputation here, so it's quite personal.

"Thanks for saying it Gus," Max gets serious, "I agree it is personal for all of us, but you're going to love this." He flips on the PowerPoint presentation and tosses case study copies on the table for them.

Max talks about how they helped the telecom industry, what they did in the real estate and insurance industries, how they worked with the industrial lubricant industry. When asked he had to admit that Big Idea didn't have a successful case study in the nuts and bolts industry. Sensing a concern about Dirk's buy-in Max quickly moves on.

He goes on to describe how they helped to transform each of the organizations in a meaningful way and how they had quantitative business performance outcomes. He showed off the kind of case studies no one ever gets, but he had them and they had done a fantastic job for those organizations.

Taking a breath, Max notices the frowning faces.

An aggravated Gus speaks up, "In the consulting and business process industry we are in Max, you guys haven't done anything. Idea Machine has been working with every one of our competitors. Are you just experimenting on us?"

Taken back by the comment, Max swallows hard. "No, this is proof that it works guys. It works in the telecom industry, the real estate industry and insurance industry, but these are just example industries Gus."

"We are not just an industry Max and you have zero proof that what you're recommending will work with TryHarder." Gus seems annoyed.

Max can feel that horrible feeling creeping in, the racing heart and cold sweat followed by nausea. *What is happening here?* As he feels his mouth dry up, he suddenly remembers his DealSMARTS℠ training. *Gus is suffering from a complete absence of belief, I've got to fix this fast.*

Recognizing he has been caught drone-a-logging Max thinks, *Gus is emotionally vulnerable right now, no wonder he is reacting negatively.* Biting his lip, Max realizes he is trying to force proof on Gus. *Just when you think you've got it the universe reminds you… you still have something to learn.*

Looking at Joe and Gus, Max pauses. "I see your point. What do you need to see to provide you the proof needed to support this internally?" Nervously he thinks, *I probably should have started with that.*

Gus leans back in his chair with a serious look on his face, "I've been thinking about it and I'm not sure, Joe help me out."

Rocking back in his chair Joe comments, "We didn't bring you in by accident Max, we have been talking about some important parts of our business and it seems like you guys have some capabilities we need. At least that is what we thought, right Gus?"

Gus raises his eyebrows, "Yeah, actually. But this happy talk about industrial lubricants may cause this thing to slip out from under us." Gus and Joe let out a sarcastic laugh.

After blinking hard, Max senses an opening and jumps in, "Why don't we isolate the capabilities and identify where there is evidence of those capabilities working." Swallowing hard he continues, "Guys, as it appears to me now, I made a mistake. I tried to show you a big picture but what you need to see is how unique this situation is. Let's look at what the core elements of our capabilities combined with yours can deliver."

Pausing for a moment Max presses on, "We are going to have to work together on this to make it a success."

Gus responds, "No doubt."

"I'm glad Max showed back up, and that Marketing hack you were impersonating is done with his happy talk," added Joe. He offers a wry smile to Max. "We want to make this deal a success, and you are going to need to help us find the way to turn these examples into things that will work here. So close that PowerPoint and get to working with us."

Feeling corrected but encouraged Max breathes deeply, allowing the nausea to subside. "First, let's talk about our process matrix." He shows them what the process matrix does, "And when used in a process like yours these are the outcomes we see." Max pulls out the case study that supports his statement.

Joe and Gus nod their understanding as they murmur, "That makes sense."

Max writes process matrix on a sticky note. "Now for our workflow engine." He repeats the process of explaining what it does and matching it with the case studies where it produced the desired outcomes.

With a noticeable change in the atmosphere of the room, Gus states, "Those are the outcomes we need!"

Max writes workflow engine on a sticky note.

For the next hour all three discuss the solution, the parts of the solutions that will make TryHarder bigger and the piece-by-piece proof in the form of outcomes.

Wrapping up the conversation Max askes, "Alright guys, what did we learn?"

Gus starts at the beginning, detailing the parts and how they fit together with TryHarder. He and Joe both discuss where there are elements of proof.

Joe frequently comments on how Small Think has demonstrated the ability to use a tool like the process matrix to achieve an outcome, adding his own internal proof. "When it comes down to it guys, the real proof this is going to work, is that we underwrite it."

Max nods eagerly, "The real proof is in this room. What do you need to see from me?"

With a stern face Gus says, "All three of us standing together Max. You need to assure us that you're going to stand here and make sure your organization delivers."

Max pauses for emphasis. "I have done that for my clients before and I will do that for you as well."

Gus and Joe agree it is essential for Max to stand behind his recommendation. Gus raises a hand to point at Max and Joe comments, "We trust you, and we will signal that to the organization. You can't let us down, OK?" Max nods, summarizes and thinks, *proof is in the eye of the beholder… has never been truer.*

"We have a plan, now we need to spec it and get it ready for budget approval." Max starts wrapping up the meeting, "is there anything else you need to see before you stand behind this package?"

"No, we're good," they chime in agreement.

"Great," Max picks up his closed computer as he continues, "we need one more meeting to create the business case before we get on the calendar with Cash."

"Good idea," Joe reacts as though he had forgotten about that, "I have a template but are you saying you can help me with that?"

"Absolutely, we want to work on that together, so we don't miss something important," Max pulls out his calendar. "Let's get that scheduled."

With the next meeting on the books, they adjourn.

Max shakes his head as he leaves the building, *I almost blew up my deal... I need to be careful with my proof.*

"Proof is like beauty - Everybody needs proof that you can do what you say you will do, but THEY determine what counts as actual proof."

- Dr. Smarts

Best Practices

High performing sales professionals do well during the WHO, WHY and WHAT components of the Discovery Phase of the sale, but the WHERE, HOW MANY, and WHERE ELSE components of the Progression Phase is where the next level of elite, high performers shine. During progression, real solutions to problems are created.

Real solutions work, and customers want proof. You have credibility, but just because you said something works is NOT proof. Even if you are an expert, the customer is not likely to believe in the solutions simply because you said it would solve the problem. World renowned Physicians with year-long waiting lists have their recommendations checked. Why would you be different?

Customers need to support their decision to adopt your solution with some sort of proof. Here's the thing about proof: like beauty, proof and value are in the eye of the beholder.

Yes, the level of proof required is situational, and it depends on the customer. Don't assume that a level of proof you want to produce is adequate or inadequate. The fact is, you don't know what will pass muster without involving the customer in the selection of acceptable proof.

If you try to develop proof too early, you're in trouble. Just to hammer this point home: you could have something that is written in the premier Journal of Universal Truths, authored by the unquestioned Truth-Sayer that everyone believes is incapable of making an error as a proof statement, but if the customer has not bought-in there will be no belief, and the proof will be inadequate. The client would say, *"well that might work in the rest of the world but here it's different."* That is the situation difference; every situation different and there is no perfect proof point.

During the development of proof, to support customers' decisions, they want to know if you have done this before, or who else you have done this with. Customers ask WHERE ELSE has this been done?

Even if you don't believe it, each customer is unique, and so is their situation. Fortunately, they don't need to see their exact situation replicated to believe in the solution. What they need to see is the most important elements of the solution or process they will be using, successfully working elsewhere.

Unfortunately, if you demonstrate an example of what the customer is looking for and you have the case studies to back it up, it still doesn't guarantee that it will work for the customer. The other part of proof, the credible belief, creates the context for the customer to make it work. Any solution can fail if it is not implemented correctly, and customers are the implementers of solution success. Customers realize the value, and that is not just a mental realization; it is an actual manifestation of the solution's value.

IF they have bought in, the customer will do what they can to make the value proposition come true. IF they have NOT bought in, they won't invest or worse, they will do what they can to support their disbelief.

It is a fact that antibiotic therapy works BUT it can fail if you don't take the pills or take it correctly. If you don't get the customer to participate in the process, knowing that it works is not good enough. Knowing what will work best for THEM is the proof.

Proof is belief more than science. You can't make baseless claims, and scientific proof helps, but it is belief that creates proof of a claim. This means that providing proof is providing support for the belief in the claim.

This is an amazing freedom you can leverage. Say you are doing something that has never been done before. The customer will still want some level of proof that it will work. If no one has done it before, do you have proof? Yes, IF the customer has the belief in the facts and thinks that they connect credibly to support their decision.

Conveying proof is NOT about finding a case study that fits, because even with a lot of enthusiasm, you can't push proof onto them. If you push proof too hard, you can destroy it. Instead, you need the customer to participate in the selection and development of the proof. It is imperative to recognize that the action in proof is where the customer develops the credible belief in the recommendation or solution; the customer is developing belief, not you.

Tangible proof is good, but even this does not hold up if they do not see some of the proof in you. Consequently, proof in the solution includes the fact that they are not alone in this. You will be there helping them succeed. If they see enough proof in your credibility, sincerity and enthusiasm, even weak tangible proof can be enough.

Also remember that customers develop the proof, which means that customers can provide their own proof all by themselves. After all, they are the ones who underwrite the decision in their organization. The proof required boils down to the capabilities to execute on the solution, BUT you can't time travel with your customer and show them the future. So, the best practice is conveying the fact that together you possess the ability to execute successfully. That means, the business case narrative of HOW the solution will work, is the strongest proof statement.

Chapter 7

Commitment WHEN

Commitment WHEN

Max prepares for his meeting with the team at Small Think. Reviewing his DealSMARTS℠ process training, he jots some notes. *I better get them to commit to a go live date, now that there is enough demand to get this deal done.*

The meeting is with Joe and Gus, but Don is still off on assignment, so he will be conferenced in. Taping his pen on the notepad Max worries for a moment. *I've been embarrassed before when the client was thinking things would happen more quickly or magically, so I'd better manage their expectations.*

Sitting at the conference table with Joe and Gus, Max welcomes Don to the meeting via conference call and everyone exchanges the usual pleasantries. It seems the weather is good at Small Think, but Don is not so lucky on location.

Starting the conversation Max begins, "Don, what are your expectations for going live with this solution?"

Stuttering a bit Don responds, "Wait... have we decided to go forward?"

"We haven't reached an agreement yet," Max acknowledges, "but as you know it takes some time for us to assemble resources and it takes the same for you. If we are going to take this project forward on TryHarder and hit your execution guidelines, we need to know when you are able to mobilize resources."

Don deflects, "Well Joe, what do you say?"

Gus and Joe talk bounces back and forth about the next steps. The people who will need to be brought in for a briefing and the executive level briefing.   Workflow consultants who need to be brought in to be trained and which people in the lab will need training. The need for a review and specification center, and a whole list of resources needed for implementation.

Max takes notes, stopping only to prompt them to include how long each step takes.

Don jumps in, "I don't care to dig into the details, but I want this to get done by the first quarter."

Gus leaps out of his chair and stammers, "Yeah but... umm... uh." Joe joins the objection chorus. "Don, it's just not feasible to get this done before the first quarter."

Don interrupts them, "Guys, listen to me. Do it in the first quarter. I said by, but I meant in the first quarter. You can do it... make it so. I need this done in the first quarter. We will increase your labor budget to make it happen. I have a revenue target I need to hit in the first half. It won't happen if we're still sputtering around in the second quarter."

Max straightens in his chair and stifles a grin to himself. "Don, can you give me an idea of what that target is?"

"We need to grow TryHarder by 10% to hit our commitment to the board in the calendar year. That means we are going to have to start HARD to be ready for our clients to pay us in the 2nd half, so we have a chance to grow by 10% for the year.

Max quickly does the calculations in his head and starts to build the end point on his business case for a return on investment. *If Don is going to grow by 10%, he will need a 10 million-dollar increase, that's some handy information I can file for later.* Don interrupts his thoughts.

"Max, with that agreement, can you deliver?" Don asks directly.

Remembering to give himself some room, Max replies, "Don, if there is any way we can - we will, but if we can't, we will let you know in plenty of time, so we can adapt, and you can update the forecast. I will take it on myself to make sure the team here gets the resources they need, but things do happen. On our end, we will do our part to make sure nothing unexpected happens, and I need your commitment to support this here."

Sounding a little annoyed, Don reiterates, "I said we would increase the labor budget, we are going to do whatever we need to do. Make this happen… I'm counting on you… all three of you."

"I'll do what I can Don," Max tries to conceal his smiles to himself again, *this is going better than I thought, my key buyer has just agreed to a go live and that we can totally do! Glad I remembered to plan for this part. THANK YOU*

DealSMARTS℠ process!

After a loud clap of thunder, and temporary silence on the line, Don exits the conversation for another call, but the meeting continues.

Max call his project manager to make introductions and discuss the particulars of the project. The project plan starts to come together as they talk about the timeline that will get them to the Go-Live date Don has demanded. They exchange contact information for continued honing of the timeline.

As Max heads to his car he thinks about the work ahead of him. *Time to prepare for my meeting with Cash. I need to build a strong business case because this is going to be a big number!*

"Expedited delivery costs more - set the go-live date and create urgency and preserve your pricing power."

- Dr. Smarts

Best Practices

Once proof has been delivered you need to put an endpoint to it and begin the process to button up the deal. The client said yes, but that doesn't mean your work is done.

Now that you are in the commitment phase, the first and most important part is to forecast outcome. Simply meaning, WHEN are you going to transfer title and have them accept ownership of the delivered product or solution. Together, you and the client need to establish a Go-Live date.

This is often left to chance because the pressures of sales deadlines have conditioned many a salesperson to charge hard for the YES on the agreement and then rest; after all you get paid based on that agreement, right? If you focus on the agreement and don't tighten up the forecast of when, you diminish your internal credibility by unnecessarily extending the timeline to get the transaction done. Worse, you may leave out some important backstops.

Backstops are critical because you want to get the transaction done as fast as possible. To do that you need to look at when they can start using the product and realizing the benefits of the solution. That is the customer's first opportunity to start realizing the value of what they've bought. Gaining revenue, reducing cost, improving quality or competitive advantage are benefits that cannot come soon enough, but they only accrue after go-live. Nailing down when go-live needs to be gives you the backstop to create a strong sense of urgency and the internal will to get the deal done more quickly.

In the proof phase, they proved to themselves they could get those benefits, so you start with WHEN they can have those benefits. It is to your benefit to remember that customers don't want the transaction, they want to get to the benefits of the solution and the transaction is how they get there.

The established Go-Live date allows you to back calculate for a smooth implementation of the solution. Usually it takes some time to build a solution, empower the team, and create the product. With this date locked, the delay between the signed agreement and the Go-Live, is an advantage for you because it creates the deliberate movement needed for the client to get the process started.

Backstops frame the set-back schedule you established in this step and that does a couple of important things. First, setting a date lets the client commit to using the product and that implies their commitment to the deal, which continues the transfer of ownership. Second, the backstop increases the accuracy of your forecast. This supports your credibility within your own company.

Remember, payday doesn't really happen when the agreement is signed. In many cases the company doesn't get paid until the final product or solution is implemented and used.

It's still up to you, but if you focus on the transaction instead of the Go-Live date, the client might be lulled into a false sense of security, that you will be doing everything for them and consequently they will under-resource the implementation.

If the client under-allocates resources, it will extend the implementation time and decrease their satisfaction. Worse, the client will blame you for the delay! So how do you avoid that?

Start with the end in mind, the Go-Live date. Then back it up and create an outline of the project. When the customer is involved in this process, you can manage their expectations and it sets the stage for the rest of the commitment phases.

Also remember, a sale is a project that needs to be managed. Effective management starts with a clear plan and ends with a fully delivered product or solution Go Live date.

Once you know WHEN they want delivery of the solution, you can manage the speed, quality, and cost equation. If they want delivery fast and cheap, they will give up quality. If they want quality but fast, that's going to cost more. Quality with a lower price tag is going to take longer.

This is the triple constraint you are always nudging speed, quality, and cost. The educated customer understands they can only have two of these.

If you do your job during the Commitment – WHEN phase, you will have better price support during the coming negotiations. Take a deep breath, you're almost there!

Chapter 8

Commitment HOW MUCH

Commitment HOW MUCH

While waiting for his appointment, Max smiles as he reads the email from Dirk Steele, the VP of Sales and Marketing at Small Think, Inc. Dirk and the human resources manager, Terri Peoples, have been working diligently behind the scenes to discuss the impact of the new solution and gather necessary information for the executive briefing. *You've got to LOVE the enthusiasm of this guy! I think I need to get him a Big Idea ball cap for his Instagram selfies. Or maybe scratch that idea. Yeah, no ball cap.*

Max collates the requested information and submits the requested documents and slides them to Dirk and Terri. He schedules a follow-up call to review the information with Dirk.

Sitting in the conference room at Small Think, Max looks over his business case in preparation. *It's all here. We have a strong rationale, and each of the solution parameters is matched to a cost of the status quo; the built in ROI is clear. Each number has been validated by Joe and Gus, and Linus has reviewed the case. The contract and justification made by Joe and Gus has been sent to leadership and Cash has received it. With Dirk and Terri preparing the executive briefing, the only thing missing is sign-off by purchasing. This is it Max, time to be a negotiation ninja.*

Joe and Max skip the usual pleasantries to grab donuts and coffee before starting their meeting. Max muses, *it's so nice when the relationship becomes comfortable enough for donuts.*

Max looks at his new friend Joe, "Everything is ready to move forward."

Sipping his coffee Joe leans back in his chair, "I've got you set up to see Cash. Everything goes through procurement. Requirement of the board."

"Of course," Max grins around a bite of donut, "We have been waiting for this day and I am really excited to meet Cash. Before I go see him, can you tell me what his goals are?"

Joe looks surprised by the question, "I have no idea Max."

"Ok, what would you say is the typical savings goal that Cash is going to ask me for? I've got to have room in the configuration to adjust on price if that's the only thing he will accept."

"Wait a second Max, what are you talking about," Joe looked concerned.

"Joe," Max explains, "in any negotiation, one person sets the configuration and the other person sets the price. We didn't come up with this price out of thin air and build in a bunch of padding, so we could negotiate away fake concessions."

Max continues, "The price we put on our products at Big Idea is the real price. That's what it's going to cost us to deliver this solution. You and I took a lot of time and effort to make sure the configuration works, so the price you're getting on this agreement is for the configuration you need."

"Now Cash needs two things," Max explains, "He needs to try and get the best price, but more importantly he needs to make sure the organization is buying the solution the right way. That means Cash is going to look at my terms and conditions, and legal disputes, and all those things, to make sure that our corporation's not trying to trick you with our contract."

Confused Joe asks, "Trick us with your contract?"

"It has happened, not with my organization but it has happened to all of us with other vendors who tried to sneak in some terms that look like a better price but let them make it up on the back end. Cash needs to know that our terms are straight, and our price is good." Max swallows the last of his donut and continues.

"I expect Cash to push on my price and you need to expect that I'm going to push back. IF he demands a better price than he will have to ask YOU what you are willing to give up. Now is there anything in this deal you are willing to give up?"

Joe becomes uncomfortable, "Honestly, I've never thought about it that way."

Max raises his eyebrows slightly, "This is essential for our negotiation planning because we can hit any price, but the configuration will change. Without saying NONE of it, when pressed what aspects of this deal are you willing to live without?"

Joe thought for a moment, "Possibly some extra training, we could do some of that ourselves. Maybe we could work with you and find a way to be more efficient with implementation hours and take some of that on ourselves."

Max takes some notes and draws some lines, pencils in some numbers. "Anything else? What about the core process workflow components of the solutions Joe, what of those are you willing to change?"

"None," Joe replied emphatically, "those are essential, and we have the proof that those are needed."

Max scribbles some more, "Okay, we can probably find a few percent here, so now my job is to go to Cash and make sure he is happy with the contract and knows he is getting a good price. When he comes to you and asks if you did your due diligence, what do you say?"

"There is nobody else in the marketplace that can help us with this solution," Joe states confidently.

Max presses a bit, "What about Idea Machine?"

"Hang on," Joe calls Gus to join the meeting for a moment. "Hey, Gus. Where are we with Idea Machine in the conversation?"

Gus eyeballs the donuts sitting on the conference room

table. "They came in and did a capabilities presentation remember? It was ALL wrong, that was about four months ago, and we eliminated them." Grabbing an old-fashioned donut and some coffee, he settles into a chair.

"Good to know," Max smiled, "Does Cash know that?"

Joe scratches his head, "Probably not," he smiles, "should we tell him?"

Max thinks for a second, *how do I want to run this negotiation? Do I want to try and surprise Cash and keep him on his heels or do I want to push straight forward?* "Joe, does Cash like to have fun during negotiations? Does he see it as a game that he wants to win, or does he try to get the deal done as quickly and efficiently as possible?"

Joe grins, "I think Cash likes the game." Gus has a mouth full of donuts but nods in agreement.

"Great, do me one favor guys, when Cash calls asking about Idea Machine, be sure to tell him what you told me about eliminating them four months ago." Max gathers his papers to head for the meeting with Cash.

Joe and Gus chime in at the same time, "Will do," Joe picks up the phone, "I'll let Cash know you are on the way."

"Wish me luck guys," Max heads out to door toward the Corporate Procurement and Supply Chain Management Department.

Making his way to meet Cash, Max thinks through some of

the details. It's the end of the month, everyone wants to do the deal and he imagines that this is an exciting part of the timing for Cash.

Max anticipates Cash will try to use the timing to his advantage and he will probably suggest there is a suitable alternative and they can shop the quote.

He also anticipates that he will be challenged on everything in the terms and conditions, including the reputation of Big Idea.

Max expects Cash will try other techniques as well, like offering things he can't deliver… such as more business or preferential treatment in other potential deals. Anything to get a better transaction on this deal.

Entering the office, Cash's assistant looks up and asks, "Do you have an appointment?"

"Cash is expecting me, Joe Balow called ahead." Max settled into the chair that the assistant pointed to.

Max takes a minute to look at the business case he constructed with Joe and Gus, the 10 percent growth rate, the $10 M revenue that Don is expecting, and the manpower resources required to meet that revenue ramp.

He notes the additional $3M in expenses required for Joe and Gus. Not to mention the time and effort required to market this by Dirk and his team for another $500,000 in effort that will go to waste.

Adding it all up for a $14.5M in economic value that could be realized if this project goes forward.

Finally, he looks at his price quote, $1.285M spent over a year - $100,000K per month for a better than 10 to 1 payback for Small Think. He thinks carefully about how he is going to position that.

Cash's assistant indicates that he is ready for Max and sends him in. Cash shakes his hand without a word and takes him to a conference table where they sit down.

Sitting with arms crossed in a power position, Cash starts the conversation, "What do you have for me?"

Max jumps right in, "You have had our contract for review and we have a proposal tied to it. Everyone has reviewed it and agrees this is the pathway forward. Now you and I need to come to an agreement between the two companies on how this moves forward."

Cash unfolds his arms slightly, "You are correct, and I apologize, I forgot you were coming in today, but I have reviewed the agreement and have a series of issues there. I have reviewed your proposal as well and we are going to need to talk about your price."

"As expected," Max replies, "where would you like to begin?"

Cash confidently launches his negotiation techniques, "Well, it's the end of the month and your price is quite high.

In fact, 40 percent higher than we can get it from another solutions provider. So, I need you to do something there, can you give me a 40 percent discount, can you do this for $850K?"

Max pauses and waits.

Cash continues talking, "If you can do that, I'm pretty sure we can get this done by the end of the month."

Max sits and waits quietly.

Cash continues, "What do you say to that?"

Keeping his wits about him, Max starts his defense. "Let's make sure we get the terms and conditions taken care of first, then we can talk about the price."

"Look. If you can't hit my price, terms are meaningless. We are not going to do this deal at your price!" Cash states emphatically.

Max remains calm. After a pregnant pause he says, "Cash, I understand your position and I will happily adjust the price as much as I can, but the terms are the deal-breaker for us. So, I need to insist that we iron out those concerns, or we will have to withdraw the offer. It's all connected, but I have very restricted latitude on what I can agree to on these terms. So please, I would like to hear your concerns there first, before we move to the price."

Cash nods in agreement and they begin to discuss and come to agreement on the terms, jurisdiction, litigation, dispute resolution, arbitration, and a variety of other situations.

Cash begins to argue about the parameters in the solution and once again brings up the price. "Now Max, understand this, we are not going to be able to afford this solution because we can get the same kind of configuration from a competitive organization. They will do it for 40 percent less than you are."

Max pauses, "Cash that's interesting, and I can see why you would want to have the best price possible but I'm pretty certain no one else can deliver this solution at this level, at a lower price."

Cash almost defiantly reiterates, "We have another supplier who will do the same thing for a lower price, you are going to have to lower your price."

Max stops and says, "Okay, I hear you. The first point I hear you saying is that you need to get a better price correct?"

Cash nods, "That's right Max."

Max continues, "The second point is you have another solution provider, correct?"

"Correct," Cash seems satisfied with the direction of the conversation.

"Let's start with that first," Max takes a breath and moves on, "Cash, I'm certain as you look at the business case you will see, there is a series of unique capabilities and solutions that cannot be delivered by anyone else, which has been validated by your team, Joe and Gus. IN fact, they assured me during multiple meetings that they understand this would be a stretch for anybody to get done and that Big Idea was the only corporation that they believed could do it."

"Well," Cash jumped in, Idea Machine says they can do whatever you can do."

Max makes eye contact with Cash, "I'm certain that they believe so, but it's not about what they believe or even about what you and I believe, it's about what Joe and Gus believe, and they believe this is the only way the solution works. If you need to, we can wait while you verify that with them."

Cash pauses and looks a little annoyed, "Okay, but I still need you to give me a better price."

Knowing he is making some progress, Max presses on. "If you look at the business case, you will see that as we looked at this configuration and these capabilities, the costs you are avoiding are significant and the revenue ramp you need to hit is substantial."

Max pauses briefly, "For us to move forward we need the right level of resources as specified in the agreement. The cost and price we put on that agreement reflects that capability. If we want to change that price, we will need to change some of the elements of the agreement."

Cash squirms in his chair and say sarcastically, "GREAT."

Max smiles, "Cash, we put the real price on that agreement, I'll give you whatever price you need to hit, but I have to take things out of the solution to do it. I don't think that is something you and I want to take back over there."

"Alright, fine," Cash relents, "but I need you to give me something!"

Pausing Max nods his agreement, "Ok, what if we extended payment terms, what if we moved the contract start date to later, what if we did some things that showed you scorable savings now but preserved the actual package price that I have approved with the organization?"

Cash looks hopeful, "Well okay, I need additional time for payments, I need another 30 days, and I need you to bill me at the beginning of the year. We'll execute the order now, you bill me at the beginning of the year, and give me an extra 30 days to pay and that is something I can take forward.

"Let me see if I can get that approved," Max jots some notes.

Cash slams the desk with his hand and laughs, pointing at Max, "YOU OLD PRO, are you kidding me? I just told you I could sign based on the terms you offered me, and you have to get them approved?"

Max smiles again, "I won't commit to what I can't deliver Cash, so if I can get that for you will we have a signed deal before the end of the month? Do we have an agreement?"

With a slight grin on his face Cash agrees, "Fine, yes… those terms, put it in an addendum to the agreement and get it over to me. I will have it signed by Friday. Get me those terms and we have a deal."

Max smiles, shuts up, stands up and shakes his hand, "Thank you for your business," then he walks out.

"Negotiation is about terms and conditions, not the price, when you have a strong value proposition."

- Dr. Smarts

Best Practices

Price is not a product attribute. Price IS the outcome of a value equation that looks like this.

Cost & Consequences of Current Situation – Cost of Solution = Economic Benefit

The old value equation was benefits minus cost equals value. But benefits are subjective and can be argued interminably. On the other hand, the cost and consequences of doing things the old way can be determined. These costs and consequences are the deficits your solution needs to fix. It's negative, not positive. The whole pile of deficits <u>minus</u> the cost of doing things the new way <u>equals</u> an economic benefit called value. That value is what you need to have the customer compare to the dollar value of your solution.

The essential part of a value based selling orientation is the recognition that price does not drive the decision.

Even though price is not a product attribute, sales people treat it as though it is. When it looks like the client is not ready to sign an agreement they think, *but what if we offered them a deal to get it done by the end of the month.* Like that will somehow modify the product to make it more valuable but in truth, they have done the opposite.

Your value proposition includes a price, and you say it as if you mean it, until you contradict yourself with a discount. You cause the customer to habituate to the idea that you are lying to them. The price is a lie. You said buy it for this GOOD price… until you confirm the lie by saying, buy it for this BETTER price. Credibility is lost. Don't let your pricing practices turn you into a liar.

If you are NOT doing your DealSMARTS℠ the right way and forget to sell value, you are sending a very bad message to your customer. In essence you are saying that you are either confused about your value proposition or are disingenuous about it.

There is no substitute for a customer's own compelling event or reason to do a deal, no substitute to mobilize action. The worst thing you can do to mobilize action before a deadline is to offer the customer a "limited time" discount if they act. The customer will recognize that you are deal prone and they will press you for more… you've told them to push hard for a better deal!

Giving in on price sounds harmless and seems like a natural part of negotiation, you probably feel like you are signaling that you want to work with them. *Here's the real price but here's your price because you're special.*

When we do this as part of the sales process, saying to the customer that this is the market price, and this is your price, you aren't being disingenuous because you have structured it as part of a deal. You stated your price to the customer, and you meant it. This is YOUR price. But, when you change that price as an incentive, you trigger the lie about the value of the product. You quoted a price you didn't mean. Your quote is not true anymore. Your value proposition is shifty.

The way to ensure you don't appear to be lying about the value proposition is to build it on top of a business case. *Here is your cost to stay put, here is my price to fix you, and here is the net cost you avoid when you do it; the value you realize.* Prices look different when tied to the business case that quantifies the cost and consequences of NOT having your solution.

When it comes to negotiations, one party sets the price, and the other sets the configuration. As the seller you have the unique privilege of going first, and you can set the price for the configuration, but the reality is, you don't set both. The customer agrees to a configuration (they set the configuration), and you offer the price for that configuration.

Buying a car is a great example of this concept. When you walk into the dealership and say, *I want that car, right there on the showroom floor,* the dealer will tell you the price of the car. The configuration is already done on the car and you are saying that you want it as is. Any other configuration will have a different price tag.

What if you only want to spend a set amount on a new car? You can tell the dealer what you are willing to spend, and THEY will tell you which cars (configurations) you can have for that price.

This is the key to a productive negotiation: remember that it is a two-party discussion. One party sets the price and the other party sets the configuration of the deal. Good negotiators and especially seasoned buyers will try to set both and drive your price down.

If the customer sets the price, then as the sales person you will need to adjust the configuration to meet that price. You don't get things for nothing in any deal. Even at Christmas the giver expects they will get a gift in return.

This is a sales best practice to adopt and remember, it is how commerce works. Master this concept or you will find yourself losing deals, even when you are the low-price bidder.

Chapter 9

Commitment WHAT NEXT

Commitment WHAT NEXT

Max walks out of the negotiation meeting with Cash and thinks, *I don't remember the last time a negotiation went like that, I really buttoned this one up!* He smiles and pumps his fist.

His DealSMARTS℠ process training comes to mind, *it was the business case and I managed my stakeholders. When Cash was trying to get some extra money out of me, like he is supposed to, he had nothing left. I'm not sure I'm happy with how easy that was.*

Suddenly he smacks himself on the forehead, *stupid, stupid, stupid, I probably left money on the table.*

Max heads back to Joe's office, "Joe, you won't believe this, but we got the deal done really fast."

"Have you talked to Linus yet... and have you followed up with Terri Peoples?" Joe seems a little concerned.

"No," Max feels a little deflated.

"We probably should do that," Joe stands up and leans on the edge of his desk.

Max starts to sit down but follows his lead and stays standing, "Why?"

Joe leans in, "I would make sure Linus is comfortable with this, because the last three deals Cash has taken up, Linus has sent back. I also heard Terri talking about staffing up and adding cost to support this implementation. THAT potentially blows up our business case, which Linus will make you wear."

Max freaks out inside and remembers that any deal can unwind and fall apart at any time. *The irony...someone who bought-in on us to protect her people, Terri Peoples, could make my deal fall APART!* He has an agreement but NOT a signed agreement yet, or even a purchase order. *This deal is not done yet.*

Rather than go crying to the parking lot, Max decides to take a risk. "Joe, can you get me in to see Linus?"

Checking his calendar Joe says, "Linus is here today and there is nothing on his schedule. Let me see." He picks up the phone and calls the assistant. "Linus is available and has some time for you Max."

A nervous feeling passes through his stomach, Max knows he is not prepared for this meeting, but he asked for it. As he enters the large suite, the assistant waves him in to see Linus, and Max sits down.

"What do you have for me?" Linus smiles but Max is not sure how sincere it is.

Max swallows hard, *I'm not prepared*, "We have just been through the negotiations of the contract to bring Bid Idea's resources into your processes and manage the redevelopment and deployment of TryHarder. We have put together a business case which supports the agreement we just reached."

Linus opens his to drawer and pulls out the business case, "This business case, right?"

"Yes, I believe that's it." Max realizes he is holding his breath and quietly releases it.

Linus nods approvingly, "It's good, that is why I let Cash go ahead and agree."

Max calms down a bit and makes a mental note, *I should have done a better of covering this base… I guess I'm lucky today.*

"You're lucky Max, I scrutinize every deal, but I like you. I like the fact you've done your job and touched all these other folks. It makes me comfortable, and not very many people make me comfortable. Most people try to come in here and sell me something and don't realize I'm here to protect the interests of the business, not buy things."

Max remembers to breath, *somehow this deal is going my direction.* His DealSMARTS℠ process training comes to mind again. "Linus, thank you for your support. I want to make sure you know we are going to stand behind our recommendations and deliver. That is WHY I'm here, to stand behind Joe and Gus and the rest of the team. Do you see anything that we have missed? What are the next steps YOU think we need to take?"

Linus looks pleased, "Part of the reason I saw you today is

that I'm going to need some financing. There are some other corporate things going on and we'd like to come to an arrangement where you can delay our first payment by 90 days and then have you bill us annually after that. Then I can budget it and we will remain budget neutral."

"Sounds fair," says Max. Luckily that still falls within his fiscal year and he'll get paid, but he makes a mental note, *I probably should have figured this out before now.* "Is there a way to get some earnest money at the beginning of this contract, so we can recognize the revenue appropriately."

Nodding in agreement, Linus replies, "We could entertain that, as long as it's digestible."

Treading carefully Max inquires, "What's digestible Linus?"

"No more than 10 percent of the face value on your agreement," Linus leans back and relaxes.

Max agrees, "Okay. Linus, what other resources didn't we consider?"

"Terri believes we will need to staff up," Linus continues, "one of the parts of your business case is a labor efficiency using your project management and work flow resources. I can't have Terri adding to my budget while I'm trying to score this budget. Do you have anything at Big Idea that can help Terri with our workforce management that can help us avoid staffing up but get more productivity out of our current people?"

Max thinks for a minute, *wow, yeah Big Idea has an HR module that is designed specifically for this.* "What if we brought some human resources technology to your organization, that would be a new project, right Linus?"

Linus considers it, "I hadn't thought about it like that but yes that would be a new project. Now remember, you need to stand behind your productivity numbers in your business case. Does this solution you're going to bring give me a net benefit above that?"

Max is careful to pick his words, "If I can verify that it will bring you net productivity above what we put in the business case, then we will bring it to you. Otherwise, I will find another potential solution for Terri. I think, but I need to verify that we can actually provide you with something that gives you additional benefits in the rest of your business, aside from the TryHarder project."

Linus smiles broadly, "Now that's a good business partner. I thought you were the kind of person we could deal with, and I'm happy to say I haven't been convinced otherwise yet."

Not sure how to take that, Max thinks, *what a strange way to say that.* He makes a mental note, *CFO's tend to cast things in a negative light.*

Max decides to take the compliment, "Thank you very much for your support." He makes a note to look at their HR module and send an email to Terri, asking for an appointment to discuss an HR idea.

Max walks back to Joe's office, "Okay Joe, that was a surprising good meeting with Linus."

"I'm glad we did this Max," Joe is visibly relieved, "I really want this project to stick. Did he say we are going forward?"

Max uses a dramatic pause, "Yes! I have some financing to arrange but we are going to get there."

"Great news," Joe grabs the phone, "Gus get in here!"

Gus extends his hand as he enters the room, "Alright, are we getting started?"

"Yes," Max shakes his outstretched hand, "the implementation team is going to be following up with you and I'm not going anywhere until we get this all square away. Then I will be checking in with you to make sure the progress happens."

Gus folds his arms, "Did you know Terri is trying to change my staff?"

"Yes, I just learned that, thanks for letting me know." Max acknowledges his concern.

Gus continues, "I can't be involved in training new people If I'm expected to get this project done. If you're going to let that happen, I can't support this deal."

Max leans back, "Calm down bud, we are going to get that handled for you."

"Okay. Make sure! I've got to get back to work because of your project timeline." Gus walks out without saying goodbye.

Max heads back to his car to make his deal notes. He calls implementation and calls the president of the company to record the sale.

What did I learn today? Max sits for a minute to reflect on the whirlwind of meetings and emotions. *I've got to cover all my bases and I needed to be looking for what's next sooner… this one almost got away from me.*

Max calls Cash one last time before heading back to the office.

Cash answers the phone, "Cash Encarey here."

"Cash, it's Max. I checked in with Linus and we are going to put some financing terms in front of you. I'd like to do that by email if that's ok with you."

Cash jumps in, "Yeah, yeah, I've already heard from Linus."

"Is there anything else I need to do for you Cash?" Max wants to make sure he doesn't miss anything else.

"Two things Max, make sure you keep me in the loop because I will need to generate a P.O. and tell me if I am reading your last name correctly."

Max laughs, "You bet, and I think so."

Cash laughs, "Your name is Max C-A-S-H-E, and you say it

cash. That means we have the same name. But also, it seems I have a last name first name. Does that make me a millennial?"

They both laugh, "Were going to have a great time working together Cash, YES, my last name is spelled correctly. I have a millennial at home, and I wouldn't peg you as one unless you're following Dirk on that Snap App. I appreciate your trust."

"Selling is cyclical - with trust you will be given more opportunities."

- Dr. Smarts

Best Practices

Once negotiation has resulted in agreement, it can feel like you are done. You did it, you landed that deal and you are home free. Hang on, you're not done yet.

There are three parts to any agreement. First, there is the

verbal agreement, where they say yes, we are going to do this. This is followed by the execution of the transaction, when they formally sign the agreement. Finally, they pay for the purchase, when the product is delivered, and the payment is received.

NOW the deal is done, the sale is made, that magic moment when the sales person has fulfilled their purpose. (Insert angels singing here!) So, What's Next?

Retailers and electronic marketers have figured this out, but it still hasn't made it into the minds of the average salesperson. The BEST time to sell something to someone is right after they have just purchased something from you.

When your customer has just made a transaction, the sale needs to be implemented and invariably in that conversation, problems occur. These problems are part of the implementation and it is your job to fix them.

Sales effectiveness is built on pain dominant logic that says, pain points are the motivating force behind a purchasing transaction. SO, when there are problems, there are opportunities to sell more stuff!

Even when the implementation goes seamlessly and once in a blue moon it will, you need to be vigilant as a professional sales person to look for other problems or issues YOU could surface and solve.

The customer that has just made a purchase from you, is the best customer to buy again, you don't have to find them and earn their trust again. Credibility is already established.

It doesn't matter what type of sale it is, it can be real estate, clothing, software or consulting services, you are always selling and developing clients for the next opportunity.

Dr. Smarts, the Dean of SMARTS University, hereby gives you permission to keep selling to that customer! Every time they see you, sell them something.

Your career depends on this habit. The difference between the professional and the amateur, the rock star and the groupie, is that the elite performing salesperson is tying together transactions in a strategic direction.

You probably hear it all the time, everyone talks about being a strategic seller, the problem is you get paid for transactions.

Sales people are inherently transactional. If you cannot rise above and think about how transactions can knit together, then you are classic, transactional sales person. You are an order taker, and a great transactional sales person, but you are going to live and die with market forces.

If your product is amazing, and your clients want it, and your price is awesome, be transactional and you'll have more business than you know what to do with, BUT the strategic salesperson will still beat you.

The strategic salesperson can go toe to toe with the classic salesperson and still beat them because they have learned to tie the transactions together. The have a customer development pathway that links them together, so the customer is not a single transaction but becomes an account.

Think about the last new client that said they were going to give you a try. They wanted you to do something for them as a pilot... and see how it goes. Did you follow up on the next transaction or did you leave it up to the client?

It's easy to get busy with other potential clients or to get stuck in implementation and forget about the WHAT'S NEXT for your customers. When you begin to think about your transactions strategically, you will start to plan for what's next in each account.

Pay attention to this as if your paycheck depends on it, because it does: there is always another offer after the sale. Don't walk away and forget the next offer.

This final part of your sales process is the beginning of the next one. Can you add start up support, workflow consulting, other products, other services, or a bigger project? What's Next?

Think about what's next, or you will work harder for less and less each year. It's up to you.

Chapter 10

Summary

Summary

Max sits at his desk and thinks about everything he learned from Dr. Smarts. *I'm going to have make sure that in each of my deals I do a proper job of discovery, manage the progression, and really think through the commitment phases. Good thing I can hold all these moving parts in my head. Next time, I will make my DealMAP℠ sooner, AND be better prepared with what I'm going to sell next.*

He contemplates his new deal. *Okay, I got this deal. They really let me run wild with this thing, good thing I had my DealSMARTS℠ structure to rely on!* **Max knows a big promotion is coming but he is concerned about what that will mean. Max thinks,** *now I better learn to manage a sales team!*

The sales team he needs to hire will be a new challenge, Max jots himself a note to follow up with DealSMARTS℠ and see what Dr. Smarts has on that subject.

He looks on the website and clicks on the Leadership Learning Pathway, and registers for his first lesson.

"The effect of a process is simple - increased predictability of your impact, timeframe, and outcome."

- Dr. Smarts

Best Practices

What have you learned from our time together? Let's recap the basics for becoming that elite sales professional!

All sales have the same basic makeup, they include three steps: discovery, progression, and commitment. Each of these steps have three phases that match up.

As you move through the steps and phases, you cover some of the same ground more than once. You make a loop and when you can match them up, you create a deal that stands on its own. That becomes your account management process.

Use a DealMAP℠, it gives the key players accountability, timelines, and outcomes, which allows you to structure the workflow and progression of the deal. It creates predictability of outcomes.

You also need the soft skills. You need to know how to ask the right questions, how to position the solution and how to make a business case. The most important of these is the business case, helping the customer come up with a tangible value to your solution.

There will be gaps in your solution or gaps in their operations that are created by your solution. These are your opportunities to find other ways to help this customer, remember the goal is for strategic transactional selling that leads to a long-term account.

DealSMARTS℠ works in simple situations, where you don't have to come up with an elaborate economic justification, just as well as it works in a commercial environment.

The commercial environments require a little more weight and heft around the demonstration, the proof, the business case, the financing, and all the other stuff. The complexity of the solution is higher, but the process is still the same.

If you apply a business case methodology, your negotiation is much easier, offering you greater opportunity to focus on what else the customer is going to need to make this deal inherently cyclical.

When you begin to make a value proposition personal, relevant to the business and concrete by monetizing it, you are adopting a value-based orientation. DealSMARTS℠ is a value-based selling methodology for engaging with the customer because of the business case focus.

Now that you have gone through this book, navigate through the DealSMARTS℠ videos and receive your DealSMARTS℠ certification on value-based selling.

Navigate to www.learn.liquidSMARTS.com to get started.

Join us again in your next learning adventure with Max and Dr. Smarts.

DealSMARTS℠

About the Authors
Dr. Gunter Wessels and Jennifer Bravo

Dr. Gunter Wessels is the founder of LiquidSMARTS. He is passionate and dedicated to the improvement of human performance and ethical business practices in sales and marketing.

Dr. Wessels leads a global practice that delivers strategic consulting and next generation personnel development services to individuals, and global corporations alike.

His expertise comes from more than 25 years in the healthcare industry, including 14 years as a consultant to global and local marketing and sales teams.

His clients gain rapid performance improvement, through the intelligent design and implementation of market approach, customer messaging communications, and sales deployment.

He leads the field in providing micro-learning for business professionals. His micro-learning approach teaches people essential soft-skills, influencing and leadership behaviors in a few minutes per day.

Dr. Wessels is the author of widely circulated articles and white papers about Healthcare Reform, Leadership, and Interpersonal Influence.

He is a sought-after speaker on the practical implications of regulatory changes, and sustaining performance during periods of industry and organizational change.

Dr. Wessels has a Ph.D. in Management with an emphasis in Marketing and Psychology from the University of Arizona, a M.B.A. from the A. Gary Anderson Graduate School of Management, and a B.S. in Biology from the University of California.

Jennifer Bravo leads LiquidSMARTS℠ as Chief Executive Officer. She ensures the company operates efficiently and that the team has the necessary tools in place to deliver quality services to their valued clients. Directing the strategy of the firm, Jennifer sets business objectives and empowers associates to achieve their goals.

Jennifer is passionate about revealing and enhancing human potential, every day she pursues her mission to improve effectiveness and performance in those around her. Her distinguished career reflects the excellence she fosters in others.

Mrs. Bravo is skilled in project management and has a wealth of operations management experience. For more than 20-years she has demonstrated excellence in leadership, financial discipline, and core business focus, leading to substantial and sustained growth and profitability.

Jennifer has consistently designed processes, facilitated change, grown bottom-line revenue, and solidified relationships in the public and private sectors. Her versatile background provides insights for efficient operations, consistent business development, and quality assurance.

Mrs. Bravo has a B.A. in Communications and Psychology from the University of Tampa and is a Certified Professional Behavioral, Motivational, and EQ Analyst.